George W. Marshall, Eng. Parish Walesby

The Register of Walesby

In the County of Nottingham - Transcribed and edited by George W.

Marshall

George W. Marshall, Eng. Parish Walesby

The Register of Walesby
In the County of Nottingham - Transcribed and edited by George W. Marshall

ISBN/EAN: 9783337192525

Printed in Europe, USA, Canada, Australia, Japan

Cover: Foto ©Andreas Hilbeck / pixelio.de

More available books at **www.hansebooks.com**

The Register

OF

Walesby,

IN THE COUNTY OF NOTTINGHAM.

BAPTISMS	-	1580—1792.
MARRIAGES	-	1594—1753.
BURIALS	-	1585—1791.

TRANSCRIBED AND EDITED BY

GEORGE W. MARSHALL, LL.D.

CONTENTS.

LONDON :

PRIVATELY PRINTED FOR THE PARISH REGISTER SOCIETY.

1898.

PREFACE.

Vols. I. and II. are thin parchment folios of the usual type, the latter unbound. The Register is in several different handwritings, and in many places very illegible. To the end of the Mariages 1636, the transcript is *verbatim* and *literatim*. The rest is a careful copy, omitting such words as "daughter of," "was baptized," &c., and placing d. for daughter, s. for son, Bapt. for "was baptized," &c.

Vol. III. is also a parchment folio, written in some places by an evidently very illiterate scribe. Inside the cover at the end is written "Mem. Fir Trees at ye Top of ye Close were given by Mr Boawre Rect^r of Kirkton ; those on ye Northside of ye Gate were planted Anno Dom^i 1733 by me, Richd Jackson, Vic^r of Walesby."

The monumental inscriptions inside the Church will be found in Jewitt's *Reliquary*, vol. xiv, page 187.

Where words are printed in *italics* the reading is doubtful owing to defects in the MS.

G. W. M.

Anno 1594.

Maried.

Willm Peck & Agnes mylnes. June 30.
John Pell & Margery mekyn. June 30.
Robt Browne & Alice mychell. Octob^r 31.
Willm Wakeden & Alice Baker. Novemb^r 17.

Anno 1595.

John foxgale and Katheryn formare. June 2.
Jarvase Henfray & *Sara.*[1] Clark. feb. 24.

Anno 1596.

Godfray Carrington & margaret Bowring. J . . .
Thomas Rawson & margret Best. August 14.
Thomas watson & margret Bradley. January 31.

Anno 1597.

Willm hopkin & Elizabeth pnell [Parnell]. August 8.

Anno 1599.

Martyn faroner & Ellyn Carrington. July 2.
Ric. Welles & Grace Rayner. July 2.
Willm Sykes & Margret Hobson. novemb^r 30.

Anno 1600.

John Waler & Agnes Burden. Aprill 1.
Thomas hurst & Ane Baker. June 19.

An. do. 1600-1. E.R. 43.

Thom: Dunston and Issabel Hirst Was maryed ye fyft daye of februarye.

E.R. 44.

Rob't shawe & margarit downes was maryed ye 31 of Januarie 1601.

An. dom. 1602.

Nicholas burdon & Joan Cresland was maryed ye 4 of July.

---

[1] Where words are printed in *italics* the reading is doubtful owing to defects in the original register.

B

Anno domine 1603.

Ric. Duecke & Eideth Ellis was maried ye 15 of maye 1603.

John Waad & Anne Hurst was maried ye 10 daye of Julye.　Anno supradicto.

James Johnson & Jane heifild was maried ye 9 of Julye 1604.

Thomas Rawood & Epham alinson was married ye 28 of october.

Thomas beedson & alis burkitt was maried ye 25 of nouember 1604.

Houghton.

Edward Wood and Anne Garnit was maried ye 27 of nouember 1604.

James meeke and Elsabeth markam.　May 13 1606.

James Wilson and Ame oldam was maried 23 of nouember.　Ann. 1606.

Henrie Renold & Gertrude Emley was maried ye 30 of nouember 1606.

Robert Leceter & Marie Tomson was maried ye 2 daye of februarie 1606.

Ric. Tod and Marie Tomson was maried ye 4 daye of maie 1607.

Thomas Mountan & Anne hind was maried ye 8 of August 1607.

John Talbott & margarit Johnson was maried ye 26 of Julie 1608.

Richard browne & Anne hurst was maried ye 30 of nouemb. 1608.

John Stuffin & bridgit hurst was maried ye 14 day of Januā 1610.

William Scikpton & marie tallbott maried ye 5 of March 1610.

francis Bridun And marie wadgdin was married ye 18 daye Jan. 1612.

Thomas Stuffin & margarit heyfeld was maried ye 31 of februarie 1612.

Thomas frogson & maude Broune maried the 27 of Aprill.　An. do. 1613.

Richard Stanfield & Rossamon Leach was maried the 9 of maie 1614.

John Butterworth & Abegall Heye was maryed the 25 of August 1614.

Thomas Sudberie & Elyzabeth baker was married the 24 of Januā 1614.

Rowland Gee of Wellow & Jane Stanfeild was maried noue : ye 18, 1615.

Henrie Bullard & Anne Burdun was maryed ye 13 of Januarye 1616.

Boughton.

Anthonye Blyth & Alis browne was maryed ye 13 of februře 1616.

Thomas Coo & Añ Stockes was maried ye 20 daye of Januarie 1617.

William tomson & Elizabeth hurst was maried ye 4 of Julie 1619.

James Bullivant & Eshabeth Tayler was maried ye 22 of october 1620.

Robart Johnson & Annis Marsh Was maried ye 30th of nouemb^r 1622.

Rob't Hurst & Annis Slined was maried y⁰ 28 of June 1624.
Rob't Townerow & Elizabeth Glined was maried y⁰ x daye of
februarie 1624.
Richard goforts & Anne Wilson was married ye Sixte of August
1626.
John Pretwell & Elyzabeth Johnson was maried y⁰ 19ᵗʰ of September
1626.
Henrie Wilson & Anne Blonke was maried y⁰ Sixtinte of nouember
1626.
Thomas Stockes & Barbara Slined was maried y⁰ 26ᵗʰ of nouember
1626.
Seth Ellis and Winnifred Browne was maried ye 28ᵗʰ of Januarie
1626.
Edward Feearebanke of Elsla[1] & Issabell burdun mar. y⁰ 4ᵗʰ of
februā 1626.
William Clifton and Agnis buller was maried the tente daie of Julie.
An. Do. 1627.
Richard gouldsberie and margerie Smith was maried the fift daye of
nouember 1627.
Thomas Cooke & Joan Haries was maried y⁰ Sixt of maye 1628.
Thomas Burden & Bridgit noble was Maried the 29ᵗʰ of June 1629.
William platts & Dowdghles Emerson was maried y⁰ first of februarie
1629.
Richard Slined & Issabell Bellamee Was Maried The fiftinᵗe day of
Julie 1630.
Oliver Howton of ollarton & Anne Hurst was maried The xxviiiᵗʰ of
Julie 1630.
James Birde and Bridget Hurst married y⁰ 14 Novembʳ 1630.
Mathew Howson & Barbara . . . . married Novembʳ 27, 1630.
James Eller & Ruthe Sleeford married January 24ᵗʰ 1631.
Nicholas Burden & Margaret Ryley were married 24ᵗʰ Feb. 1631.
William Clifton & Dorothy Hardy were married Novembʳ 23ᵗʰ
1632.
Thomas Milles & Jane Welles were married Decemb. 1ᵗʰ 1632.

Anno 1633.

Richard Nicholson & Alice Taylor were married June 17ᵗʰ.
Wittm Alcocke & Anne Johnson were married y⁰ 11ᵗʰ of Septembʳ.
John Colte & Anne Appleby were married y⁰ 22ᵗʰ of Septembʳ.

Anno 1634.

Symon Cooke & Mary Browne were married July 17.
James Freeborrowe & Ellen Bilby were married Novemb. 1⁰.
John Ragge & Sarah Bradshaw were married Novemb. 11ᵗʰ.

Anno 1636.

Francis Shipton & Sence Short were married novembʳ 1⁰.
Frauncis Moody & Margaret Thorpe were marryed Novemb. 20ᵗʰ
1638.[2]

[1] *i.e.*, Elksley.
[2] End of page 5 of Register. So far this is a literatim copy.
B²

Baptisms.

1580. Georg f. michale Omley [Emley].   Dec. 4.
       Issabell f. Lawren. Michock.   Feb. 23.
       Margreta f. Ric. spery.   Mar. 23.
1581. Joan f. Thome lighe.   May 1.
       Issabell f. Cuth. Eme^{r}sŏ.   Aug. 4.
       Katheryn f. xp̄o Blarfoth.   Feb. 7.
       Ric. f. Talbt Baker.   Mar. 17.
       Eliz. f. Mychaell Emley.   June 20.
1582. Ric. f. Ric. hurst.   Aug. 25.
       Olyve f. Will'm soufing.   m^r 17.
1583. Eliz. & Mary daughters of Law . . .   Oct. 28.
       Georg. f. Cuth. Eme^{r}son.   Oct. 29.
       Alice f. Edm'd greene.   Feb. 1.
       Margret f. Thome Johnsŏ.   Feb. 27.
       Edmund f. Johis Whyt.   Mar. 25.
1584. Ric. f. Thome Brone.   Mar. 29.
       Pet^r f. Ric. spery.   July 1.
       Margery f. Thome lighe.   Aug. 9.
       Kathary f. Law. Bretton.   Oct. 18.
       Gartryd f. mychaell Emslye.   Mar. 12.
       Bridget f. Rich. hurst.   Mar. 21.
1585. Thom. f. Thom. Browne.   Sep. 28.
1586. Raffe f. Cuth. Taylor.   May 8.
       Archiball f. Rob't Bullar.   Jan. 26.
       Robt. f. Ric. hurst.   Feb. 14.
       Agnes f. Law. mickock.   May 20.
       Thom. f. Will'm Stuffinge.   June 20.
       Ellyn f. Thome fowler.   July 30.
       Ric. f. Tho. ouldam.   Aug. 11.
       Rob't f. John Aukley.   Aug 14.
       Rob't f. Archibald Harbr̃son.   Oct. 16.
1587. Hennery f. Rob't bullow.   Aug. 8.
1594. Agnes f. Rob't Bullow.   Feb. 18.
       Agnes f. Johañs Clark.   June 2.
       Rob't Wakeden.   June 2.
       John f. Thome Brown.   July.
1595. Agnes f. Rob't Browne.   Jan. 26.
       Ric. f. Henery we . . .   Jan. 30.
       Agnes f. Joyce Symson.   Mar. 1.
       Jane f. Will'm Peck.   Mar. 19.
1596. Agnes f. Thome Bordan.   Apr. 25.
       Agnes f. Thom. stoakes.   June 14.
       Agnes f. Symond Cook.   June 29.
       Abigail f. Law. hey.   Nov. 2
1597. Rob't f. sam̃eli Johnson.   Apr. 30.
       Agnes f. John vrst [? for Hurst].   May 19.
       Rob't f. Will'm Pecke.   .   .   .   .
       Rob't f. Rob't Stoakes.   Nov. 14.

1597. xpopher f. Cuth. Emeʳson. Nov. 25.
1598. Thomas f. Richard's Stoakes. Apr. 9.
Deborah f. Law. hey. Apr. 14.
Alice f. Agnes habʳson. Apr. 25.
Thomas f. Thome Bordon. May 7.
Eliz. f. James Johnson. Sept. 17.
Jane f. Will'm Sharpls. Oct. 2.
Thomas f. Will'm Bower. Feb. 18.
1599. Law. f. Law. Bretten. June 17.
Ric. f. Ric. foster. Aug. 12.
Charles f. E . . . . *Stuffing.* Dec. 23.
Gartrid f. humfry Taylor. Jan. 13.
1600. Nicholas f. George hargreave. April 13.
Talbott f. Law. Hey, May 24.
Agnes f. Will'm Sykes. May 24.
Thomas f. Joh'is foxgale. June 1.
Will'm f. Will'm Bower. July 16.
Avis f. Franciscus Whyt. July . .
Rob't f. Thome hurst. Sept. 26.
Susan f. Cuth. Emerson. Oct. . .
John s. Symon Coulte. 12 Oct.
Judith d. Thomas Stocks. 19 Oct.
Anne d. Ryc. foster. 16 Nov.
Godfrae [and] James sonnes of James Carrington. 27 Feb.
1601. Susanna d. James Johnson. 9 May.

Christening from Boughton.

1600. A dau'r of george Furnis. 30 May.
1601. Alithia d. John Waler. 3 Aug.
Thomas s. Roger Sliforth. 13 Dec.
James s. Thomas burden. 10 Jan.
Rychard s. Antonie hurst. 17 Jan.
Thomas s. Ric. foster. 24 Jan.
1602. Thomas s. thomas Hurst. 2 Sept.
Simon s. Simon Couke. 12 Sept.
Will. s. Will. Hurst. 3 Oct.
Samuel s. Mʳ Heye. 21 Oct.
John Warde & margarit children to John Warde. 31 Oct.
Halis d. John strongarme. 14 Jan.
Andrewe s. George Argreffe. 13 Mar.
1603. Izabel d. nicholas Burdon. 3 April.
Willi. s. thom. Hurst. 6 Nov.
Thomas s. thomas stoockes. 18 Dec.
Margarit d. will. hurst 5 Feb.
1604. Halis d. Ric. Duecke. 14 Aug.
John s. Roger sliforth. 13 Jan.
Robt s. Anthonie hurst. 3 Feb.
Britgit d. John waler. 13 Feb.
Henrie s. Simon Couke. 17 March.

1605.   Edward s. John Clarke.   14 May.
        Millisant d. Thomas Stockes.   20 May.
        Anne d. Tho. beesonn.   8 Sept.

                        Boughton.

1605.   Willi. s. Rob't browne.   17 Nov.
1606.   Will. s. Tho. browne.   6 April.
        Robert s. Nicholas burdon.   27 April.
        Anne d. Ric. hurst.   14 June.
        Joel s. Roger Gliforth.   12 July.
        Samuell s. William Sharples.   12 Oct.
1607.   Ric. s. Rob't Leceter.   24 June.
        Bredgit d. Anthonie hurst.   18 Oct.
        William s. William hurst.   28 Oct.
        Thomas s. Thom mountan.   1 Nov.
        Richard s. Richard hurst.   30 Nov.
        Thomas s. John talbott.   21 Dec.
1608.   Ric. base s. anne hurst wedoe.   5 Aprill.
        Gilb't s. Thomas baker.   5 June.
        Anne d. Thomas mountaine.   25 Dec.
        Judith d. John Talbott.   19 Jan.
        Margarit d. nicholas burdun.   22 Jan.
1609.   Elyzabeth d. Richard hurst.   7 April.
        Ruth d. Roger Sliforth.   15 April.
        Thomas s. Ric. browne.   28 Jan.
1610.   Marke s. Rob't leceter.   25 April.
        Milisant d. William Wood.   20 May.
        John s. William sharples.   15 July.
        John s. John Talbott.   19 August.
        Halis d. Anthonie Hurst.   8 Sept.
        Dorathy d. James Wilson.   29 Sept.
        Thomas s. tho. baker.   17 Feb.
        Francis d. John Jeneuer.   10 Mar.
1611.   John s. Richard cam.   6 July.
        Tho. s. Ric. hurst ye younger.   28 July.
        Francis s. Thomas mountan.   29 Jan.
1612.   Elyzabeth d. John talbott.   3 Oct.
        Elyzabeth d. nicholas Burdun.   20 Dec.
1613.   Elyzabeth d. Tho. Stuffin.   1 May.
        Henrie s. Rob't leaceter.   2 May.
        Thomas s. William sharples.   30 May.
        John s. Mr Smyth.   26 Sept.
        William s. Anthonie hurst.   17 Oct.
        Dorathy d. Willi. baker.   18 Oct.
        Henrie s. James Wilson.   14 Nov.
        John s. Richard hurst.   21 Dec.
        Anne d. John Talbott.   12 Feb.
        Marie d. Will. Wood.   13 Feb.
1614.   Richard s. Thomas Mountan.   22 May.
        Jane d. Mr Smith.   14 Dec.

1614. Robart s. Richard hurst. 19 Feb.
1615. Ric. s. William ferriman. 11 May.
Anne d. Robert Leaceter. 25 June.
Bridgit d. Nicholas burdun. 19 Nov.
Edmond s. John Talbot. 17 Dec.
Marie d. George Emerson. 3 March.
Thomas s. Robert heyfeld. 24 March.
1616. John s. Mr Smith. 19 Feb.
Lowrence s. henrye Bullard. 22 Feb.
1617. Anne d. Willyam Wood. 10 Aug.
James s. Thomas Mountan. 13 Nov.
William base s. Ollife wlles *(sic)*. 9 March.
Edmond s. Thomas Baker. 23 March.
1618. Margarit d. James Wilson. 15 April.
Richard Stanfield s. Richard. 3 May.
francis s. Marke short. 7 June.
Robart s. Henrie Bullard. 17 Jan.
Rob't s. Richard Hurst. 21 Feb.
Ric. Coult s. John. 28 Feb.
Margaret & Marie frebora. 20 March. subposed father
    Richard Hurst.
Frauncis d. majester Smith. 25 April.
1619. Thomas s. Thomas heapes. 15 Aug.
George s. William Tomson. 3 Oct.
Ellys s. Rob't heyfeld. 6 Feb.
1620. Elizabeth d. George Emerson. 17 April.
Elizabeth d. William Wood. 17 April.
William s. Richard platts. 1 Oct.
Anne d. Marke Shorte. 11 Dec.
Elizabeth d. Thomas Mountan. 6 Jan.
Thomas s. Henrie Buller. 28 Jan.
Barbara d. James Wilson. 2 Feb.
1621. Margarit d. Ric. hurst. 10 June.
Grace d. William Tomson. 17 June.
Richard s. Robert Brown. 21 June.
Richard s. Thomas Baker. 31 Augt.
Margarit d. Mr Smith. 9 Sept.
Milisant d. Thomas Heapes. 12 Oct.
Samuell s. John mottram. 11 Nov.
1622. Rozamon d. James Bulleuant. 8 Sept.
Rob't s. Rob't Johnson. 6 Jan.
Richard s. Richard Platts. 24 Nov.
Robart s. Robart Heyfield. 2 Feb.
Frãcis s. John appelbie. 16 March.
1623. frances d. Marke Short. 11 Jan.
Cutbert s. Thomas Bulliuant. 28 Jan.
Robert s. John Coult. 14 March.
1624. James and Brydgit children of Richard Hurst. 12 July.
William s. Mr Smith. 25 July.
francis d. henrie Buller. 25 July.

John s. Edward barlow. 2 Aug.
francis d. Thomas mountan. 19 Sept.
Marie d. Rob't Johnson. 25 Sept.
John s. Thomas Woollas. 8 Oct.
Joan d. Walter Ireland. 28 Nov.
Barbara d. Willi Wood. 12 Dec.
Edward s. Margerie Truswell. 16 Dec. The supposed
    father Charles Watmouth.

1625. Elyzabeth d. Thomas heapes. 3 April.
Tho. s. Rob't hurst. 15 April.

Anno 1585. Sepul^r.

1585. Katheryn ux. Thome Arklye. 20 June.
Eliza. f. Law. mycock. 7 Aug.

1594. Will'm mecock. 15 Jan.
Eliz. leighe. 1 March.
Ane West. 14 March.
John fereven. 19 March.

1595. Ma⌐gret Brandam. 26 Aug.
Rob't Wakden. 30 Aug.
Edmund Whyt. 13 Nov.
margret Leighe. 12 Jan.

1596. Jane Peck. 31 March.
Joane ux. Thome Waler. 16 April.
Agnes f. Joyce symson. 21 Sept.
Ellyn f. Symond Cooke. 14 Nov.
Ane f. Symond Cook. 26 April.
Alice f. Rob't Stoakes. 4 May.
Will'm f. James Johnson. 11 May.
Margaret ux. Will'm spadman. 26 Aug.
Xpofer f. Cuth. Emerson. 17 March.

1597. Henery West. 2 April.
Thomas Cossyns. 13 April.
Margery Lalam. 21 April.
Rob't Stoakes. 10 May.
Ric. f. henery West. 4 June.
John ouldham. 20 Sept,
Lettis freeborow. 4 Jan.
Thomas Barlow. 15 Feb.
Agnes f. Rob't Browne. 11 March.

1598. Rob't f. Rob. stoakes 6 July.
Alice Dewike. 8 Nov.
Elizabeth Elley. 14 Nov.
Will'm hopkyn. 17 Dec.
Eliz. vx. Will'm hopkyn. 25 Dec.
Thom. f. Will'm Bowe⌐. 22 Feb.
Agnes ux. James meeke. 22 March.

1599. Thom̃s f. Thome Stoakes. 17 April.
Jane f. francis Whyt. 2 July.
Grace Lewis. 23 Oct.

1599. Gartrud f. humfrye Tayler. 23 Jan.
1600. Ric. Allynson. 6 Sept.
     Mowd wyfe Rob't Wareng. 17 Oct.
     Elyzabeth ye hirst[1] Widoe. 28 Oct.
     Thom. s. Simon Couke. 22 Nov.
     John foxgale. 29 Nov.
     Thom. Rowson. 21 Dec.
     Anne d. Ric. foster. 14 Feb.
1601. Talbot s. M^r heye. 6 April.
     Henrye Waler. 13 April.
1602. Issabel w. of thom. burdon. 6 May.
     Judith stockes d. Thom. 29 Sept.
     Thomas s. Thomas hurst. 31 Oct.
     John s. John Ward. 9 Nov.
     Margarit d. John Ward. 14 Nov.
     Joan wife of John Ward. 17 Dec^r.
     Margarit Hett. 22 Dec.
     Rob't dodson seruant to Ryc. hurst. 8 Jan.
     George stuffin. 14 Jan.
     Alycia d. John ferim. 21 Jan.
     Willi. s. Willi. hurst. 5 Feb.
     Edith Duicke. 10 Feb.
     Gertrude vx. Jakobe Johnso[n]. 21 Feb.
1603. Samuel s. M^r heye. 23 June.
1604. Ann wife of James Carrington. 6 April.
     Thomas Stopworth Seruant to Sr John Hollis. 20 June. A
         Burieng from houghton.
     John s. Roger Sliforth. 21 Jan.
     Izabel wife of John needom. 14 Feb.
1605. Elizabeth Tayler. 23 Aug.
     Thomas Hurst. 29 Oct.
     Tho. burkitt. 3 Jan.
1606. Auis w. of Gilb't Baker. 11 Oct.
     Sences wife of Cutbert bouth. 17 Dec.
     Simon Couke. 8 Feb.
1607. Gilb't baker. 2 Aug.
     Thomas s. Thom. Mountan. 14 Nov.
     Ric. s. Ric. hurst. 12 Dec.
     Thomas s. John talbott. 17 Jan.
1608. Richard s. Anne hurst. 20 July.
1609. Thomas Claye. 9 May.
1611. John Waler. 6 Dec.
     Jarvis henfre. 12 Jan.
     Rychard s. Thomas Stoockes. 7 Feb.
     John Jenever. 26 Feb.
1612. Cutbert tayler. 23 July.
     Milisant d. william Wood. 6 Sept.
1612. Thomas burdun. 14 Sept.

---

[1] *See* name " Hurst " below and in other places.

1612. Thomas s. Thomas Browne. 31 Oct.
Thomas hurst. 18 Jan.
Margarit Jenever, wedoe. 6 Feb.
Agnis wife of William Stuffin. 22 Feb.

1613. Laurentius Heyes Clericus huius Ecclesiæ vicarius. Natu
Lancastriensis, obijt in Domino Junij 13.
francis s. Thomas manton.[1] 11 July.
John filius Edmundi Smithe clerici & istius ecclesiæ vicarij
sepultus Septemb^r 29.
Elyzabeth wife of James Meecke. 12 Oct.
John s. Richard hurst. 24 Jan.
James Meeke. 19 Feb.

1614. Thomas burdun. 25 April.
Henneri s. Robert Lecetor. 24 June.
William baker. 12 July.
William Truswell. 24 Feb.
Rob't s. Richard hurst. 26 Feb.
Thomas base s. Jane Summersets. 10 March.
Johnie Hankocke. 22 March.

1615. Elizabeth wife of Richard Chadwicke. 30 Sept.
Thomas Rowood. 14 Jan.
Robart Browne of boughton. 21 Jan.
Katharen Stuffin. 22 Feb.
Howes Tayler. 13 March.

1616. Ellyn hurst wedo. 27 March.
Houmfra tayler. 17 April.
Margarit Best. 1 May.
Anne ouldam wedo. 1 May.
francis Bridon. 2 May.
Thomas s. John Coult. 9 Aug.
francis d. John Jenever. 27 Oct.

1617. Grace wife of Richard Weler. 18 Oct.
Epham wife of Thomas Rowood. 20 Dec^r.
Lowrence Bretten, Clarke, 4 Feb.
Marye wife of Richard Tod. 17 March.

1618. Ric. s. Ric. Stanfield. 7 May.
Lowrence s. henrie Bullerd. 19 July.
Thomas Baldin. 18 Aug.
Annis wife of Richard hurst. 4 Dec.
Elyzabeth d. homfra tayler. 25 Dec.
Marie Bauldin. 10 Feb.
Marie wife of Richard houlmes. 21 Feb.

1619. Margarit wife of John talbott. 12 April.
Henrie Barlow. 25 May.
Anne pecke vid. 28 Nov.
francis s. marke Short. 7 Jan.

1620. George s. William tompson. 7 May.
Richard Welles. 7 Feb.

[1] Manton is written above Thomas. Manton=Mountain. See baptism 1611-12.

1620. Richard Browne. 20 Feb.
1621. Thomas Browne. 8 Jan.
1622. Anne Waler vedeo [widow] 25 March.
James s. Thomas Mountan. 10 Oct.
Oughton. John Billidge. 15 Oct.
Edith wife of Richard Dueike. 25 Nov.
Olife d. Thomas Bullivants. 20 March.
Archibald s. Rob't Buller. 24 March.
1623. Richard s. John Coult. 10 April.
Barbara Houmes vedeo. 16 July.
Joan Burden vedeo. 17 July.
Anne d. Robert browne. 25 July.
Robert s. Robert Browne. 12 Aug.
Robert browne the father of the said child. 16 Sept.
Elizabeth s. Thomas Mountan. 2 Oct.
Cutbert s. thomas bullivant. 29 Jan.
James Wilson. 11 March.
1624. James s. Richard hurst. 13 July.
Bridgit d. Ric. hurst. 18 July.
Edmon Smith, Clarke. 17 Oct.
Grace d. John Browne of Ramton. 8 Nov.
Ann wife of george Emerson. 20 Nov.
Marie d. Robert Johnson. 18 Dec.
An pernell. 28 Dec.
Edward base s. margerie trusswell. 29 Jan.
A poore man Called John Herall. 8 Feb.
Margarit wife of Rob't Buller. 12 March.
Thomas Butterworth of tuxforth. 15 March.
1625. Elyzabeth Truswell video. 10 April.
Elizabeth barlow video. 11 May.
Margarit d. M^{tris} Smith. 8 July.
Marie Breedon video. 20 Oct.
francis d. Henrie Buller. 15 Nov.
Thomas Johnson. 23 Nov.
Grace wife of Cutbert Emerson. 18 Jan.
Thomas Riche. 17 Feb.
Elizabeth d. Thomas Heapes. 12 Feb.
1626. Cutbert Emerson. 10 April.
Anne Johnson video. 2 June.
Milisant d. Thomas Stoockes. 17 Aug.
xpofer s. Edward barlow. 12 Oct.
Anne d. Rob't hurst. 19 Jan.
Elizabeth d. Richard hurst. 22 Jan.
1627. Marie d. marke shorts. 17 April.
Rob't s. John Coult. 23 April.
Andrew Hunt, Lowcuntrie souldior. 13 Dec.
1628. M^{ster} Edmond Suttun, Gent. 18 April.
Archibald s. henry buller. 9 May.
Richard s. Richard Gosforth. 18 May.
Margarit d. Thomas Heaps. 3 July.

Baptisms.

A christening from Boughton 1625. Anthonie s. Ric. Browne. 27 Nov.

1625. Raphe s. Rob't Johnson. 11 Dec.
Barbara d. Jonathan tayler. 19 Feb.

1626. Richard s. George Emerson. 21 Feb.
Margarit d. Thomas bullivant. 26 Feb.
Thomas s. John Appelby. 4 March.
Christofer s. Thomas Moughton. 3 March.
Xpofer s. Edward barlow. 12 March.
Rob't s. James bullivant. 31 May.
Archibald s. henrye buller. 24 Sept.
Anne d. Rob't hurtes. 31 Dec.

1627. Edmond s. William hurst. 24 May.
Ric. s. Ric. goforth. 22 July.
Margarit d. thomas Heapes. 29 July.
Margarit d. m^{a}ter Henrie Truman. 17 Jan.
Marie d. Rob't Hurst. 26 Jan.
Dowdghles d. George Emerson. 31 Jan.

1628. Elizabeth d. Rob't Johnson. 12 April.
Thomas s. Thomas Stoockes. 1 May.

1629. James s. Henrie Buller 12 April.
Rob't s. Marke Short. 21 June.
Rob't s. William Clifton. 4 Oct.
Henrie s. m^{ter} Henry Trwman. 17 Dec.
Halis d. Thomas Coukes. 6 Jan.
francis d. Thomas Stoakes. 17 Feb.
Ruth d. Ric. Leaciter. 21 Feb.
Tho. s. Rob't Johnson. 24 Feb.

1630. Rob't s. Rob't Hurst. 1 Aug.
Elinor d. willi. platts. 5 Dec.
William s. willi. Hurt. 23 Jan.

1631. Boughton. William s. Ric. Browne of Boughton. 1 May.
Eelizabeth d. John Buttries. 18 Sept.
Bridget d. James Bird. 25 Feb.
Elnor d. Henry Cooke. 2 March.

1632. Margaret d. Thomas Stokes. 2 May.
John s. Henry Trewman, Clerke. 29 May.
Mary d. Rob't Johnson. 24 June.
Jane d. Richard Hurst. 2 Aug.
John s. Rob't Hurst. 2 Aug.
Thoñs s. Mathew Howson. 12 Aug.
Elisabeth d. Peter de May. 24 Aug.
Jane d. Richard Leicester. 24 Oct.
Thom's s. Thom's Cooke. 21 Dec.
Alice d. Nicholas Burder. 17 Jan.
James s. John Gyniver. 1 March.

1633. Jane d. Thomas Fosken. 3 April.
Henry s. Henry Cooke. 14 April.

1633. Elizabeth d. Wm Hurst. 26 June.
Thomas s. Joel Sliford. 27 Sept^r.
1634. Henry s. John Buttery. 16 April.
Henry s. Thomas Stokes. 10 June.
Anne d. William Alcocke. 7 Aug.
William s. Richard Dewicke. 14 Sept.
William s. Mathew Howson. 27 Sept.
Thoms bastard s. Joane Woodcock. 28 Sept.
Anne d. Henry Trewman, clerke. 3 Oct.
Richard s. Rob't Hurst. 12 Oct.
Jane d. Richard & Elizabeth Slynhend. 24 Nov.
Ann d. Christopher & Grace Hather. 11 Feb.
1635. Thomas s. Nicholas Burden & Margaret his wife. 13 June.
Richard s. Thomas Milne & Jane his wife. 29 Aug.
John s. Richard Hurst & Katherine his wife. 4 Sept.
Elizabeth d. James Freeborowe & Ellen his wife. 20 Oct.
164.. James s. Freebara & Elin. 29 Feb.
1652. William s. Laurence Wombell & Isabell his wife, of Walesby.
18 Oct.

Burials.

1628. Joan wyfe of Thomas Slined. 17 Jan.
Ric. Tod. 11 March.
Edward Arnall. 13 March.
1629. Seth Ellis. 28 March,
George Emerson. 7 April.
Edward Slined of Gamston. 20 Oct.
Elizabeth wife of William Hurst. 9 Nov.
John Baker of Houghton. 16 Nov.
Raphe Marsh. 23 Dec.
Ric. s. Marke Short. 24 Feb.
Francis d. Thomas Slined. 23 March.
1630. Rob't Heyfield. 5 April.
Joan Browne wedeo. 31 July.
Rob't s. Rob't Hurst. 7 Aug.
Margarit wife of Thomas Stoakes. 15 Aug.
Halis wife of Ric. Houlmes. 19 Sept.
Margarit d. William Hurst. 10 Oct.
Elizabeth wife of Ric. Hurst. 12 Oct.
Joan wife of Nicholas Burdun. 22 Jan.
Ric. Duecke. 24 Feb.
Elyzabeth wife of Marke Short. 13 March.
1631. Hales Couke. 5 April.
Willfra Hurst, 19 April.
Olde Kyelling of Mauncefield. 24 April.
Tho. s. Robert Johnson. 30 April.
Ruth d. Richard Leasiter. 12 May.
Marke Short. 20 May.
Ric. Hurst ye Elder. 14 July.
Roger Sliforth. 7 Aug.

1631. Jane wife of James Johnson. 11 Nov.
       Robert Buller. 12 Dec.
       Mary wife of John Colt. 7 March.
1632. Anne wife of Richard Goeforth. 29 March.
       Gertrad Brittan. 10 May.
       Elnor d. Henry Cooke. 12 May.
       Isabel wife of Richard Slynhead. 17 May.
       Isabel wife of James Bullivant. 18 May.
       Isabel wife of William Wood. 4 June.
       Henry Buller. 5 June.
       Thomas Heapes. 15 June.
       James Johnson. 7 July
       Anne wife of Will'm Clifton. ⎫ 14 July.
       Margaret d. Richard Hurst.   ⎭
       Will'm Stuffin. 20 July.
       Anthony Hurst. 24 July.
       Jonathan Taylor. 30 July.
       Barbara d. Jonathan Taylor. 14 Aug.
       Anne & Rob't Welles. 21 Aug.
       Elizabeth d. Peter De may. 24 Oct.
       Rob't Johnson. 3 Novr.
       John Appleby. 7 Dec.
       Widowe Marshe. 13 Dec.
       Jane d. Will'm Wood. 2 Jan.
       William Wood. 11 Feb.
       James s. John Gyniver. 2 March.
1634? Elizabeth d. Wm. Hurst. 30 June.
1634. Anne Butler. 16 June.
       John Stuffin. 31 Aug.
1636. Richard Slynehead. 25 March.
       Mary d. William Hurst & Anne his wife. 5 Feb.
       Tho. s. Joel Sleeford & Elizab{h}. his wife. 6 Feb.
1637. Edward s. William Hurst & Anne his wife. 10 June.
       Anne d. James freeborow & Ellen his wife. 24 July.
       Thomas s. Nicholas Burden. 17 Nov.
       Dorothy d. Rob't Johnson. 26 Feb.
1638. Mary d. Rob't Leceter. 14 April.
       Richard Nicholson. 19 April.
       William Stuffin & Wm ye son of William Awcock. 5 Oct.
       Luce wife of Francis Bankes. 18 Oct.
       Thom's Slynet. 17 Nov.
1639. Bridget d. Henry Parre. 27 March.
       Elizabeth ye wife of Joel Sleeford. 7 April.
       Elizabeth the wife of Edward Hynd. 16 May.
       Thomas Mountayne, 19 March.
1640. Henry s. Thomas Stokes & Barbara his wife. 4 April.
       Katherine Fosken. 5 May.
       Henry Parre. June.
       George s. Peter Demay. 7 Aug.
1641. Robert Hyfield . . . .

Weddings.

1639. William Johnson and Anne Parre. 28 Nov.
1640. Roger Flintham and Alice Hy . . . . 30 May.
1641. Robert Rawson and Bridget . . . . . 20 May.
Richard Mountaine and Ann *Dewicke*. 10 Feb.

Vol. II.

I James Edlar Registar for Walesbey since the 11 day of November 1653.

Roberde s. Roberd Rawsone and Brihgit his wife bapt. 17 Nov. 1653.

Elizabeth d. Christopher Fostar and Anne his wife bapt. 27 Nov. 1653.

Winnifrid Ellise buried 22 Dec. 1653.

Mary d. Richard Mountaine and Mary his wife, bapt^d . . Jany 1653.

Elisabeth wife of humphray haye buried . . Jany 1653.

Elisabeth Wawing buried . .

Mary d. John . . Bapt. 15 Feb. 1653.

Rodgar s. Rodgar flintorne and Allis his wife. Bapt. 24 Feb. 1653.

Anno dommini 1654.

Katrine d. John Clarke and Rosa . . his wife, bapt. 28 March.

Susand Johnson. Buried 3 April.

John duffe. Buried . . April.

Rowland Fostard of Boughton. Buried . . .

Ann wife of Willyam Banes. Buried 25 May.

Whinefride wife of henrie Cooke. Buried . . June.

ghearge Abell of boughton. Buried.

Godfray s. Godfray Newham and Frances his wife. Bapt. 16 July.

George s. Richard Collingham and Jane his wife bapt. 2 Sept. 1654.

Willyam s. Willyam Berand and Margrit his wife bapt. 17 Sept. 1654.

Ruthe wife of James Edlar. Buried 21 Sept.

Willyam Bannes buried 10 Nov. 1654.

Richard s. Richard Pettinar and dorite his wife. Bapt. 8 March.

Anno dommini 1655.

Thomas s. John kelot buried *12* April 1655.

John s. John kelot and Ellnar his wife bapt. 16 April 1655.

Ellnar wife of John Kellot buried 28 April 1655.

—rie d. Godfray Newell buried 21 May 1655.

frances d. Godfray Newell, buried 26 July 1655.

Alice d. John Clarke and Rosamond . . . bapt. 26 Nov.

. . . d. Ellies Hifelde and Christan . . . bapt. *26* Dec.

Mary d. John Walker and Anne his wife, bapt. 14 March 1655.

John s. John Berrey and Milld his wife, bapt. 10 April 1656.

Ellisabeth d. Richard Milnes and Jsbell his wife, bapt. 23 Sept. 1656.

Willyam s. Robarde Rawsone and Bridgit his wife, bapt. 29 Oct. 1656.

francese d. Godfray Newham and frances his wife, bapt. 1 Nov. 1656.

John s. Rodger flintam and Alse his wife, bapt. 4 Nov. 1656.

Marey d. Richard Alcocke and Elinar his wife, bapt. 14 May 1656.

Jane d. John Butturrei and Alse his wife, bapt. 17 May 1656.

John s. Willyam Berand and Margit his wife, bapt. 31 May 1656.

Willyam s. Marey Browne, bapt. 13 July, 1656.

Marsey d. Ellisabeth Foskewe, bapt. 20 Dec. 1656.
Ellisabeth d. John Kellat and Anne his wife, bapt. 30 Dec. 1656.
John s. John Clarke and Marye his wife, bapt. 4 Jan. 1656.
Anne d. Richard Collingham and Jane his wife, bapt. 15 March 1656.
John s. Willyam Hurste and Alse his wife, bapt. 19 March 1656.
Isbel d. John Clarke and Rose his wife, bapt. 26 March 1657.
Anne d. Francis Bamford and Liddia his wife, bapt. 24 Sept. 1657.
Anne d. Godfraye Newham and frances his wife, bapt. 11 Decr 1657.
John s. Henry Cooke and Elisabeth his wife, bapt. 3 July 1658.
Thomas s. Richard Milnes and Isbel his wife, bapt. 15 Sept. 1658.

> James Freebaro, Regester.

Alaes d. John Clark and Maray his wife, bapt. 28 Feb. 1659.
Maray d. Antoni haye and maray his wife, bapt. 4 March 1659.
Maray d. Ellies hifilde and Cristan his wife, bapt. 22 May 1659.
Ann d. James Walkar and Rosamond his wife, bapt. 25 May 1659.
Mara d. Willim parken and maray his wife, bapt. 14 Aug. 1659.
Thomas s. Martan Whit and Esebell his wife, bapt. 9 Sept. 1659.
Maray d. Roger flentom and Alce his wife, bapt. 10 Sept. 1659.
Jane d. Tomas Cooke and Jane his wife, bapt. 16 Sept. 1659.
Thomas s. Willam Wiat and doraty his wife, bapt. 18 Sept. 1659.
Saray d. Gorg nora and Elisebeth his wife, bapt. Oct. 1659.
John s. John Berrey and millay his wife, bapt. 19 Oct. 1659.
Maray d. John Coult and grace his wife, bapt. 6 Nov. 1659.
Maray d. Willam Robards and Elisebeth his wife, bapt. 18 Nov. 1659.
Maray d. Robard Roson and bridgest his wife, bapt. 12 March 1660.
Thomas s. Thomas Stokes and Jahen his wife, bapt. 18 March 1660.
Elin d. Richard Olkot and Elin his wife, bapt. 27 March 1660.
maray d. Richard millnes and Esebel his wife, bapt. 8 April 1660.
Thomas s. Thomas Smith and Eliesebeth his wife, bapt. 3 July 1660.
Franses s. Franses Johnson and Margat his wife, bapt. 2 Sept. 1660.
Frances s. Frances Johnson and margat his wife, bapt. 9 Sept. 1660.
Ane d. Martin White and Esbel his wife, bapt. 30 Sept. 1660.
Elesebeth d. James Wolkar and Rosemon his wife, bapt. 7 Jan. 1661.
Anne d. John Clarke and maray his wife, bapt. 16 July 1661.
Jane d. Godfray nuem[1] and franses his wife, bapt. 4 June 1661.
Cornelas s. Cornelas bishep and maray his wife, bapt. 25 July 1661.
Elias s. Elias hifild and Cristan his wife, bapt. 25 Augt 1661.
Maraye and Elesebeth d's of Robert Atkin and his wife, bapt. 14 Oct. 1661.
Lorrance s. Lorranes Wombell and Elesebeth his wife, bapt. 24 Oct. 1661.
Jone d. Tomas Cooke and Franses his wife, bapt. 28 Feb. 1662.
Elesebeth d. Thomas nihelson[2] and Elesebeth his wife, bapt. 2 March 1662.
Brigat d. John Coult and grase his wife, bapt. 9 March 1662.
Thomas s. Rogar Flintom and allse his wife, bapt. 5 April 1662.
Elisebeth d. Thomas Stockes and Jane his wife, bapt. 9 May 1662.
Maray d. —bard Shay[3] and Elisebeth, bapt. 26 June 1662.
Dinas and John sons of Dinis Rachfild and Alce his wife, bapt. 31 Oct. 1662.

---

[1] i.e., Newham.   [2] Nicholson, *vide* post.   [3] Robert Shaw.

C

Burials.

1656.	March	2.	Jone wife of Thomas kooke.
	May	16.	Willyam Browne.
	June	29.	Judith wife of Abraham . . . . .
	Oct.	25.	Ollive Bullivant.
	Nov.	28.	frances d. Godfray Nuham.
	Dec.	30.	Ellisabeth d. John Kellat.
	Dec.	31.	Jane d. John Butturri.
	Jan.	8.	John s. John Clarke.
	Feb.	17.	John s. Willyam Berand.
	Apr.	1.	Ellisabeth de May.
	Jan⁷	10.	Christian d. Ellise Hifelde.
1657.	Oct.	8.	Anne wife of francis Bamford.
	Dec.	8.	Ellisabeth Duicke.
	Dec.	10.	Marie bastard of Ellisabeth Foskew.
	Dec.	14.	Jane wife of Martaine White.
	Dec.	2.	Allis Hifelde, widdow.
	Jan.	13.	Grace Harrise, widdow.
	Feb.	5.	Frances d. Martan White.
	Feb.	19.	John Clarke.
1658.	April	3.	Willyam Welles.
	April	6.	Dorritie Clarke.
	April	21.	Anne Akooke widdow.
	April	30.	Ralfe Johnson.
	May	5.	Rodgeer and John sons of Rodger flintam.
	May	6.	Elisabeth foskew and John Berrie.
	May	14.	Anne wife of John Coulte.
	May	14.	Anne Allcocke.
	May	20.	Barbara Allcocke.
	May	21.	Anne wife of John Clarke.
	May	29.	Elisabethe d. James freeburrow.
	June	3.	Margit wife of William harker.
	June	15.	John s. John Gredggary.
	June	16.	Allis wife of Nicklis Knight.
	June	25.	John Gredgrie.
	June	27.	Dudglowes¹ Lecitar.
	June	29.	Anne wife of John Walker.
	June	29.	Willyam s. Goodfreye Newham.
	July	9.	James Ellar.
	Aug.	5.	Anne Cooke d. Henrye Cooke.
	Oct.	17.	Henrye s. Henrye Cooke.
	Nov.	5.	Thomas s. Richard Milnes.
	Dec.	5.	Gonae Pare.
	Dec.	28.	Barbaa wife of Matew Henson.
1659.	April	29.	Richard Collinggam.
	Aug.	8.	Cattran horest.
	Sept.	9.	Tomas s. martan white.

¹ *i.e.*, Douglas.

1659.	Aug.	12.	Cattaren wife of Antanni blithe.
	Sept.	16.	Jane wife of Thomas Cooke.
	Oct.	9.	Robard Bollay.
	Oct.	22.	Anne d. Richard Collinggam.
	Nov.	16.	Maray d. John Coult and grase his wife.
	Nov.	24.	The wife of Robard greey.
	Nov.	25.	Alce d. John and Maraye Clark.
1660.	Feb.	82(sic).	Ellin d. Linatel Wolker and Ann his wife.
	March	7.	Henray Cooke.
	April	. .	John Clark.
	June	24.	Maray wife of Willam Parr.
	Oct.	3.	Robard s. Robard horst.
	Dec.	17.	Franses s. frances Jonson.
1661.	Jan.	27.	John nicklnson.
	Mar.	1.	Thomas hifeld.
	May	10.	Richarde s. Marten White.
	Sept.	23.	Alce Reuel.
	Oct.	6.	Alce hourst.
	Nov.	. . .	Maray wife of Willam Parkin.
1662.	Feb.	5.	Eline d. Rogar Flitam.
	Feb.	14.	Christifoth hathar.
	April	26.	Nathen s. Fraunces Johnsonne.
	Oct.	18.	Auies d. John Clarke and Maray his wife.
	Nov.	2.	Dinas and John Rachfild.
1663.	Jan^y	30.	Christon wife of Elies hifeld.
	Feb.	27.	maray d. John Wollker.

Weddings 1654.

Willyam Bearand and Margrit Stoakes, 28 March.
Thomas Walker and Anne Colton, 28 November.
Daniall Dunston and Elisabeth Browne, 30 January.

1655.

Willyam pitche and Jsabell Beridge, 8 May.
George Buttree and Ann Button, 24 May.
Richard Milnes and Jssabell Rocklaye, 13 Nov^r.
Humphray Hay and Katrine Gilbard.
Anthoni Hay and Marie Clarke, 29 Jan.
John Berrie and Millisant Heapes, 11 Feb.
John Kellot and Anne Milnar, 10 March.
francis Wooddas and frances Stoakes, 21 Nov. 1656.
Henery *Poole* and Elisabeth Tate, . . . Feb. 1656.
Willyam Hurst and Alice Cooke, 15 Sept. 1656.
Willyam dobson and katrine Hay, 6 April 1658.
John Gredgary and Marie Fooxe 10 Nov. 1651 (? 7).
Thomas Stoakes and Jane Nickcolson, 13 April 1658.
John Wolker and Elisabeth Shawe, 28 Nov. 1658.
Willyam Wiate and Dorrataye *Pettenary*, 30 Nov. 1658.
Thomas Cooke and Jane white, 14 Dec. 1658.

C²

John **Coulte** and Grase gaskin, 3 Feb. 1659.
John llooson[1] and Ampllates . . . April 1659.
Thomas Smith **and** Elisebeth Reme*p*, May 1659.
Thomas Housonn **and** Ruth hifild, 12 May 1659.
John Borckby **and** Ann Rotar, 18 May 1659.
Willam Coupar and maraye garad*m*, 24 May 1659.
Thomas Whitlam **and** Elesebeth Blithe, 3 March 1660.
Richard Worslay **and** Maray grevay, 24 Oct. 1660.
John **bottara** and Roseman Simson, 27 Nov. 1660.
Bee it remembered that vpon the 11th Day of November 1658 James
   Freeber of Walesby came before mee and tooke his oath to be
   prish Register of y⁰ sayd towne. I do approve hereof. Given
   under my hand at Grove the day & yeare aboue written. Edw.
   Neville.
John Selles **and** Elin more, 22 Oct. 1661.

1663.

John s. Martin white and Isabell his wife, bapt. 7 April.
James s. James Walker and Rosamond his wife, bapt. 19 May.
Katherine Clarke widdow, buried 9 June.
Robert s. Robert Atkin and Mary his wife, bapt. 18 July.
Mary d. William Wyat and Dorothy his wife, bapt. 4 Aug.
Thomas s. Thomas Nicolson and Elizabeth his wife, bapt. 20 Sept.
Thomas Cooke and Margaret Makin, married, 17 Aug*ᵗ*.
Robert Parre, buried, 5 Dec.
Thomas s. William Lupton and Elizabeth his wife, bapt. 5 Jan*ʸ*.
Elizabeth d. Edward Dent and Ellen his wife, bapt. 14 Feb.
John and Elizabeth the s. and d. John Clarke and Mary his wife,
   bapt. 14 Feb.
Elizabeth d. John Clarke and Mary his wife, buried, 26 Feb.
Ellen wife of Edward Dent, buried, 6 March.
John s. John Clarke and Mary his wife, buried, 20 March.

1664.

Henery s. Thomas Stokes and Jane his wife, bapt. 27 March.
Anne d. Thomas Cooke and Fraunces his wife, bapt. 30 April.
Anne d. William Parre, buried, 14 May.
Ellen d. John Clarke and Rozamond his wife, bapt. 17 Aug.
Anne d. Thomas Cooke and Margaret his wife, bapt. 18 Sept.
Frauncis s. Robert Shaw and Elizabeth his wife, bapt. 2 Oct.
John s. John Colt and Grace his wife, bapt. 16 Oct.

1665.

John s. Colt *(sic)*, buried, 12 April.
Godfrey Nuham, buried, 27 May
Edward Bulley and Anne Woolla, married, 15 June.
Mary d. Thomas Nicolson and Elizabeth his wife, bapt. 18 June.
Elizabeth wife of Thomas Nicolson, buried, 16 July.
Jane d. Richard Milles and Isabell his wife, bapt. 23 July.

---

[1] ? Hooson.

Thomas s. Roger Flintam, buried 30 July.
James s. Lawrence Womble and Elizabeth his wife, bapt. 6 Aug⁴.
Mary d. Thomas Nicolson, buried, 7 Aug.
Christopher s. John Clarke and Mary his wife, bapt. 3 Sept.
Anne wife of Edward Bulley, buried, 18 Oct.
Thomas s. Thomas Hawson and Ruth his wife, bapt. 18 Oct.
Edward Dent and Alice Duffi, married, 14 Nov.
John s. Edward Dent and Alice his wife, bapt. 27 Feb.
Georgius filius populi et Dorothæ Jackson, bapt. 28 Feb.
Thomas s. Christopher Mountane and Barbara his wife, bapt. 4 March.
Ann d. Ellis Hifield and anne his wife, bapt. 7 March.
Sarah wife of Thomas Clark, buried, 13 March.
Ann d. Ellis Hifield and Anne his wife, buried, 23 March.

1666.

Thomas s. Richard Smith, buried, 17 May.
Katherine wife of John Mee, buried, 25 May.
William Hall, buried, 30 July.
Jane wife of Thomas Milles, buried, 7 July.
Frauncis s. Thomas Stokes and Jane his wife, bapt. 26 Aug.
James Wiswould of West Markham and Alice Burdon of Walesby, married, 21 Oct.
Mary d. John Colt, bapt. 25 Oct.
Henry Parr and Frances Hall, married, 19 Nov.
Samuell Atkins of Clifton and Joannah Hurst of Walesby married 22 Jan.
Robert s. Will. Hurst of Walesby, bapt. 17 March.
Katharine d. Tho. Rashley, bapt. 24 Feb.
John Colt, buried, 16 Sept. '67.
James s. James Freeborrow, bapt. 22 April, '67.
Thomas Nicholson and Alice Wallhead, married 6 June, '67.
John Heath and Elizabeth Cooke, married, 11 June, '67.
Anne d. Robert Shaw, bapt. 16 June, '67.
William s. William *Idy*ott, bapt. 11 Novʳ '67.
Mary d. Edward Bully, buried, 23 Nov. '67.
Thomas Milles, buried, 29 Nov. '67.
Anne d. Richard Milles, bapt. 8 Dec. '67.
Anne d. John Heath, bapt. 22 Dec. '67.
Edward s. Edward Dent, bapt. 2 Feb. '67.
Robert s. Lawrence Woombell, bapt. 9 Feb. '67.
Widow Burden, buried, 19 Feb. '67.
Elizabeth d. Ellis Hyfield, bapt. 19 April '68.
John s. Edward Dent, buried, 22 April '68.
John Buttery, buried, 1 May '68.
Geaorge hinde, buried, 5 May '68.
Thomas Heapes sepult. Sept. 4.
Millysant wife of John Berie, buried Sept. 15.
. . . wife of Anthony Pick, buried Oct. 3.
. . . wife of James Walker, buried Nov. 24.

. . . d. Thomas Nicolson, buried Dec. 26.
. . . wife of Thomas Nicolson, buried Dec. 26.
· · · · · · · · · · · · Feb. 7.
· · · · · · · · · · · · Feb. 20.
John Berrie & Eliz. Buckles married . . .

1669.

Mary d. Robard Rawson and Bridgit his wife. Buried May 13.
Mary d. Robard Shaw and Elzabeth his wife. Buried May 23.
Ann d. Willyam hurst and Mary his wife. Buried Aug. 13.
Thomas Taylar and Ann Flintam. Married June 20.
Thomas Michill and Ellinn Freeburow. Married July 1.
Mary wife of Richard Mountan. Buried Aug. 30.
Richard s. Thomas Taylor and Ann his wife. Bapt. Aug. 30.
Widdow Pich. Buried Sept. 20.
Barbara and Jane daũrs of Thomas Stoakes and Jane his wife. Bapt.
    Nov. 21.
Elizabeth Nickolson, Widdow. Buried, Dec. 3.
John Worslay of dunham and grace Coult. Married Dec. 21.
John Walker. Buried Jan^y . .
Elizabeth d. John Berry & Eliz. his wife. Bapt. Jany 11.
William Wyat. Buried, Jany 18.
Elizabeth wife of John Berry. Buried Jany 20.
Margaret d. Will. Parre. Buried Jany 31.
James s. Lawrence Womble. Buried Feb. 24.
John Clarke of Willowby. Buried March 6.
Anne wife of William Hurst. Buried March 16.
Roger and Richard sons of Willm Hyfeild & Mary his wife. Bapt.
    March 18.

1670.

Mary d. Thomas Michel & Elliner his wife. Bapt. April 9.
Lawrence Wombel. Buried, April 18.
Thomas s. Robert & Brigett Rawson. Buried May 1.
Robert Shaw. Buried, May 21.
George s. Martin and Elizabeth White. Bapt. May 23.
George s. Martin and Eliz. White. Buried May 30.
Matthew Howson. Buried Aug. 24.
Ruth d. Tho. Pashley & Alice his wife. Bapt. Aug. 30.
Ellin d. Eliz. Wombel Wid. Bapt. Sept. 30. Buried Oct. 1.
Barbara d. Thomas Howson. Buried, Oct. 6.
Robert s. William Beiron & Margaret his wife. Bapt. Nov. 20.
Mary Wells, Widd. Buried Dec. 21.
Roger s. William and Mary Hyfeild. Buried March 2.
Thomas s. Willm Hurst jun. Bapt. March 5.
Abraham ye Bastard sunn of Jane Marshall. Bapt. March 19.

1671.

Troth wife of Willm Parkinson. Buried March 13.
Thomas Pashley. Buried, April 28.

An d. Willyam Womble. Buried June *3.*
Richard s. Henry Whitlam & Ester his wife. Bapt. June 28.
Richard Hyfield. Buried Octr 24.
Robert Rowson. Buried Oct. *15.*
Ann wife of Nicolas Knight. Buried Oct. 18.
Alce *Dus* widd. Buried, Oct. 25.
Richard s. Richard scot. Bapt. Nov. 1.
Ruth d. Thomas houson. Bapt. Dec. 21.
John s. Thomas stokes. Bapt. Jan. . .
John Worsley & Elizabeth Sha. Married Dec. 22.
Jone d. John Heath and Elizabeth his wife. Bapt. . .

1672.

John s. Thomas Stokes and Jane his wife. Buried March 16.
John s. Marting White & Isbell his wife. Buried Aug. 4.
Elizabeth d. Willyam parkinson. Buried June 17.
Richard s. heneree Whitlame and Easter his wife. Buried 9 Aug.
Elesebeth d. Wilyam hifeeld and Mary his wife. Bapt. 16 Aug.
Anne d. Thomas michele and Elene his wife. Bapt. 11 Sept.
Elizebeth *neler.* Buried, 25 Sept.
Anne d. Thomas michel and Elene his wife. Bapt. 3 Oct. *(sic).*
John s. John Worsla and Elesebeth his wife. Bapt. 6 Oct.
Robard Alkoks buried Dec. 22.
Stephen s. Willyam berend and margeret his wife. Bapt. 29 Dec.
Stephen s. Willyam berend and margeret his wife. Buried 14 Jan.
Elesebeth d. John berree. Buried 16 Jan.
James[1] s. Thomas Stokes and Jane his wife buried 14 Feb.

1673.

James s. James Walker. Buried 27 March.
. . . Freebora. Buried 6 April.
John s. John hurst and Mary his wife. Bapt. April.
Eliz. d. George Flintham & Anne his wife. Bapt. May 29.
Eliz. d. Henry Whitlam & Ester his wife. Bapt. Oct. 12.
Tho. s. William Leyceter & Elianor his wife. Bapt. Nov. 3.
Tho. s. Thomas Michel & Elianor his wife. Bapt. Nov. 23.
George s. Jo. Berry & Mary his wife. Bapt. Jan. 11.
Mary d. Will. Cooke & Anne his wife. Bapt. Mar. 1.
Richard s. John Hurst & Mary his wife, buried . .
. . . Flintham, buried April 21.
Mary wife of Willm Hurst. Buried Jan. 12.
Edward Feerbanke & Alice Lund of Boughton. Married Apr. 29.
Joshua Martin and Mary Barker. Married May 29.

1674.

Jane Lylliman. Buried April 10.
Willm Hurst, jun. & Eliza Scot. Married May 7.

1 ? Thomas.

1675.

William s. William & Mary Heyfield. Bapt. Decr 19.
Ann d. William & Ann Cook. Bapt. Jan. 5 1676.
Richard s. Thomas and Jane Stoakes. Bapt. Feb. 20 1676.

1676.

Elizabeth d. Thomas Mitchall. Bapt. May 16.
John s. John Hurst. Bapt. June 11.
Robert s. Richard Scot. Bapt Oct. 27.
Simon s. of William Lecitor. Bapt. Oct. 28.
Mary d. Henry Whitlam. Bapt. Nov. 5.
Richard s. William Hurst, jun. Bapt. Jan. 11.

1677.

Robert s. Robert Parkinson. Bapt. July 16.
John s. John Clark. Bapt. Sept. 29.
William s. William Cook. Bapt. Oct. 9.
John s. Richard Simpson of Boughton. Bapt. Dec. 11.
Charles s. Charles Warrener. Bapt. Jan. 5.

1678.

William s. Hen. Whitlam. Bapt. July 21.
Mary d. Edward Moore. Bapt. Aug. 11.
Elizabeth d. Robert Parkinson. Bapt. Aug. 13,
Elizabeth d. John Worselay. Bapt. Oct. 22.
James s. Thomas Mitchell. Bapt. Dec. 22.
William s. John Clark. Bapt. Feb. 2.
Frances d. Richard Milnes. Bapt. March 16.

1679.

Jane d. Godfrey Newham. Bapt. Aug. 9.
Lydia d. Thomas Stoakes. Bapt. Nov. 5.
Elizabeth d. Will. Cook. Bapt. Nov. 13.
Thomas s. Will. Heyfield. Bapt. Feb. 1.
Margret d. Richard Scot. Bapt. March 21.

Married.

William Harrison and Allice Pashlay. Nov. 21, 1675.
Charles Warrener and Catherine Marshall. Nov. 16, 1676.
Edmond Elyot and Elizabeth Unwin. June 26, 1677.
William Harrison and Ann Boynby. June 15, 1680.
Thomas Taylor and Elizabeth Sadler. Aug. 26, 1680.

Burials 1676.

Rosamond wife of John Clark. June 18.
Mary d. Mary Whitlam. Nov. 10.
Ann d. John Heath. Dec. 2.
Nicholas Knight, senex. Dec. 4.

1677 (Burials).

Christopher Hather.   April 3.
John Heath.   May 1.
Elizabeth Hinde, wid.   Aug. 15.
Hen. Newham.   Dec. 27.

1678 (Burials).

Thomas Howson.   April 12.
Elizabeth d. Rob't Parkinson.   Sept. 6.
William Hurst, sen^r.   Oct. 29.
Simon s. Wm Leciter.   Jan. 14.
Mary d. Wm Leciter.   Jan. 16.
Barbara wife of Thomas Stoakes sen^r.   Jan. 25.
Robert Rawson.   Feb. 13.
Allice wife of Wm Harrison.   Feb. 14.
William s. John Clark.   Feb. 27.
Elizabeth d. Thomas Mitchell.   March 1.
Mary d. Thomas Mitchell.   March 14.

1679 (Burials).

William Parkinson.   March 28.
Robert Hurst, senex.   March 29.
Frances d. Richard Milnes.   April 12.
Thom. s. Christopher Mountaine.   April 14.
Hellen Allcock, wid.   July 10.
William s. Henry Whitlam.   Aug. 12.
Jane d. Godfrey Newham.   Aug. 18.
Hellen Freeborrow, wid.   Sept. 18.
Mary wife of John Berry.   Nov. 17.
Lydia d. Thom. Stoakes.   Dec. 1.
Elizabeth wife of John Worselay.   Dec 23.
Ann Mountaine.   Jan. 1.
John Berry.   Jan. 19.
Esther wife of Hen. Whitlam.   Feb. 6.
Ann wife of Thom. Tayler.   March 15.

Vol. III.

Anno Regni Regis Caroli secundi &c. Tricesimo secundo. Annoq'
Domini 1680.   Wm Pennington Vic.

Walesby Christenings 1680.

Mary d. Robt & Ann Parkinson. Sept. 15.
W^m s. John & Ann Clark. Sept. 26.
Godfrey s. Godfrey & Ann Newham. Oct. 10.
W^m s. W^m & Hellen Lecitor. Dec. 21.
Ann d. W^m & Ann Harrison. March 20.

1681.

Thomas s. Thomas & Elizabeth Taylor. April 27.
Ann d. W^m & Elizabeth Hurst. July 14.
Ann d. Charles & Catherine Warrener. Dec. 25.
Hellen d. Thomas & Hellen Mitchell. Jan. 21.
Mary d. Robt Parkinson & Ann his wife. Feb. 16.

1682.

Thomas s. W^m & Mary Hyfield. April 9.
William s. W^m & Elizabeth Moss. July 23.
Jane d. W^m & Ann Cook. Oct. 29.
Robt s. John & Ann Clark. Jan. 4.
Frances d. John & Jane Bacon. Jan. 21.
Ann Bastard child of Mary Baxter. Feb. 2.

1683.

John s. Thomas & Elizabeth Taylor. March 25.
John s. W^m & Ann Harrison. April 5.
Henry s. Godfrey & Ann Newham. June 15.
John s. W^m & Hellen Lecitor. June 30.
Mary d. Charles & Catherine Warrenr. July 12.
Ann d. Wid. Scot. July 12.
Rose d. John & Ann Hyfield. Dec. 23.
Thomas s. Thomas & Hanna Stoakes. Feb. 5.

1684.

Mary d. John & Elizabeth Hurst. April 12.
Elizabeth d. W^m & Elizabeth Moss. April 13.
Francis s. Robt & Ann Parkinson. Aug. 17.
Cuthbert s. John & Jane Bacon. Nov. 23.
John s. Hen. & Rosamond Whitlam. Jan. 6.
William s. W^m & Ann Cook. Feb. 22.
William s. Godfrey & Ann Newham. March 11.

1685.

Francis s. Thom. & Hellen Mitchel. Aug. 18.
Jane d. John & Jane Bacon. Dec. 25.
Margret d. W^m & Elizabeth Moss. March 19.

1686.

William s. John & Elizabeth Hurst. May 9.
Mary d. Godfrey & Isabel Smith. Aug. 15.
Mary d. Godfrey & Ann Newham. Nov. 3.
William s. W^m & Ann Harrison. Jan. 24.
Elizabeth d. John & Ann Hyfield. Feb. 8.
Mary d. William Pennington, Vic., & Mary his wife, born Feb. 22,
 bapt. March 8.

1687.

Sarah d. Charles & Catharine Harson. Aug. 18.
James s. W^m & Hellen Lecitor. Sept. 1.
Elizabeth d. W^m & Ann Cook. Nov. 1.
Mary d. Thomas & Catharine Wyat. Dec. 20.
John s. W^m & Elizabeth Moss. March 6.

1688.

John s. Thomas Mitchel. Nov. 2.
Richard s. John & Ann Hyfield. Nov. 7.
William s. Jarvise & Margret Hill. Dec. 12.
Ann d. Godfree & Ann Newham. Feb. 16.
Mary d. John & Elizabeth Hurst. March 24.

1689.

John s. W^m & Ann Harrison. June 27.
Elizabeth d. Wm Pennington, Cler. & Mary his wife, born Sept. 30,
 bapt. Oct. 9.
Elizabeth d. W^m & Jane Prestwood. Nov. 26.
Joan d. Richard Bean. Nov. 29.
Catharine d. Thom. and Cath. Wyat. Dec. 13.
Elizabeth d. Thom. Mitchel. Dec. 25.
William s. Will'm & Elizabeth Parkin. Feb. 4.

1690.

Henry s. John & Jane Bacon. April 21.
Mary d. Wm Moss. June 25.
Elizabeth d. Richard & Ann Wright. Aug. 26.
Jane d. Charles & Cath. Harson. Jan. 16.

1691.

Thomas s. William & Ann Harrison. April 15.
Elizabeth d. Jarvise & Margret Hill. Oct. 25.
Mary d. William & Mary Moss. Feb. 20.
John s. Richard & Mary Bean. March 15.
Elizabeth d. W^m & Elizabeth Parkin. March 17.

1692.

William s. Thom. & Catherine Wyat. Apr. 24.
Thomas s. John & Elizab. Hurst. April 24.
Henry s. Henry & Elizab. Stoakes. May 17.
Susanna d. Godfrey & Ann Newham. Sept. 24.
Ann d. Thomas Mitchel. Dec. 20.
Mary bastard child of Sarah Butcher. March 8.
Ann d. John & Jane Bacon. March 19.

1693.

Thomas s. Will'm Parkin. April 14.
John s. Christopher & Mary Clark. Jan. 3.

1694.

Catherine d. Charles & Cath. Harson. Oct. 28.
Thomas s. Thomas & Catherine Wyat. Jan. 1.
William s. Thomas Mitchel. Jan. 18.

1695.

Mary d. Richard & Mary Bean. April 14.
Jane d. Henry & Elizabeth Stoakes, born May 12, bapt. June 11.
Richard s. William Harrison & Ann his wife, born June 13, bapt.
    June 22.
Philip s. Thomas & Susanna Mountaine, born June 19, bapt. June 25.
Richard s. William & Allice Parkin, born Sept. 29, bapt. Oct. 2.
Elizabeth d. John Bacon & Jane his wife, born Jan. 18, bapt. Feb. 16.
John s. William & Ann Couper of Budby, born Feb. 3, bapt. March 1.

1696.

Elizabeth d. John Hurst & Elizabeth his wife, born March 24, bapt.
    April 19.
Samuel s. Christopher & Mary Clark, born June 13, bapt. June 19.
Martha d. Christopher & Mary Clark, born June 13, bapt. June 19.
Jane d. Richard & Elizabeth Newland, born June 12, bapt. July 10.
Hugh s. Thomas Mountaine & Susaña his wife, born Nov. 4, & Bapt.
    Dec. 2.
Robert s. Thomas Mitchel, born Feb. 10, bapt. March 14.

1697.

Jane d. Thomas Wyat & Catherine his wife, born April 6, bapt.
    April 13.
George s. George Cam, born April 13.
Jarvise s. Jarvise Hill & Margret his wife. born & bapt. Aug. 30.
John s. Jarvise Hill & Margret his wife, born & bapt. Aug. 30.
Ann d. John Par & Allice his wife, born Sept. 5, & bapt. Sept. 19.
Hanna d. Henry Stoakes & Elizabeth his wife, born Sept. 12, bapt.
    Sept. 17.
William, s. James Cam, born Nov. 16.
Philip s. Wm Lecitor & Elizabeth his wife, born Dec. 29, bapt. Jan. 2.
Ann d. Thomas Justice & Ann his wife, born Feb. 5, bapt. Feb. 12.
Elizabeth d. Richard & Elizabeth Newland, born March 18, bapt.
    March 24.

1698.

Mary d. William & Ann Harrison, born June 26, bapt. July 3.
Allice d. Godfrey & Ann Newham, born Aug. 9, bapt. Aug. 13.
Christopher s. Christopher & Mary Clark, born Sept. 14, bapt. Octr 16.
Frances d. John & Elizab. Hurst, born Dec. 29, bapt. Jan. 16.
Luke s. Thomas Mountain, born Jan. 24, bapt. Jan. 31.
Benjamin s. Richard & Mary Bean, born Feb. 2, bapt. March 19.

1699.

Jane d. Thomas & Katherine Wyat, born & bapt. April 4.
Elizabeth d. Thomas & Katherin Wyat, born & bapt. April 4.
Thomas s. John & Barbara Winterbottom, born & bapt. May 30.
Mary d. Thomas & *Cath*. Mitchel, born 8 bapt. 15 Oct.
John s. John Par & Allice his wife, born 12 bapt. 19 Oct.
Elizabeth d. Thomas & Ann Justice, born & bapt. Nov. 12.
James Cam Child was born Feb. 14, which died before it had a name given.[1]

1700.

Robert s. Robt & Barbara Daft, born April 5, bapt. April 12.
Mary d. William & Elizabeth Lecitor, born April 13, bapt. April 14.
William s. Godfree & Ann Newham born April 12, bapt. April 19.
Frances d. Thomas & Catharine Wyat, born Aug. 22, bapt. Sept. 5.
John s. Richard & Elizabeth Newland, born Nov. 29, bapt. Dec. 13.
Phebe d. George Cam, born Dec. 27.[1]
Jonathan s. James Cam, born March 4.[1]

1701.

Robert s. John Par, born April 3, bapt. April 8.
Mary d. John Winterbottom, born June 20, bapt. June 21.
William s. Christopher Clark, born Jan. 7, bapt. Jan. 8.

1702.

Elizabeth d. Godfrey Newham, born May 6, bapt. May 19.
Allice d. John Par, born July 8, bapt. July 13.
Robert s. Robert Daft, born July 9, bapt. July 19.
John s. John Hurst jun^r, born Feb. 18, bapt. Feb. 20.
William s. Edward Shepherd, born Feb. 22, bapt. March 22.

1703.

Elizabeth d. Edward Eagle, born April 17, bapt. May 19.
Thomas s. Thomas Justice, born April 24, bapt. May 3.
John s. John Winterbottom, born & bapt. Aug. 1.
William s. John Winterbottom, born & bapt. Aug. 1. *(Vide* 1784).
Joseph s. Edward Roe, born Aug. 22, bapt. Aug. 29.
Joseph s. Christopher Clark, born Sept. 6, bapt. Sept. 18.
Elizabeth d. Thomas Wyat, born Dec. 23, bapt. Jan. 20.

[1] Probably Quaker's hence no date of Baptism, *vide* entry of conversion of a Jonathan Cam, *post.*

1704.

Ann d. John Hurst, born & bapt. March 27.
Dennis s. Godfrey Newham, born April 6, bapt. April 30.
Anne d. Richard Newland, born April 17, bapt. May 16.
Thomas s. John Leary, born Sept. 12, bapt. Oct. 8.
Sarah d. John Winterbottom, born Oct. 11, bapt. Oct. 12.

1705.

George s. Robert Daft, born April 20, bapt. April 28.
Ann d. Edward Roe, born May 25, bapt. June 4.
Sarah d. Tho. Justice, born June 14, bapt. June 26.
James s. Christopher Clark, born March 16, bapt. March 21.

1706.

Sarah d. William Brunt, born April 5, bapt. May 5.
George s. Samuel Story, labourer, born & bapt. Aug. 26.
Henry s. Thomas Whitlam, Couper, born & bapt. Dec. 29.

1707.

Timothy s. Christopher Clark, husbandman, born May 26, bapt.
    May 31.
Elizabeth d. John Winterbottom, born July 20, bapt. Aug. 16.
Sarah d. Richard Newland, labourer, born July 31, bapt. Aug. 4.
James s. John Leary, husbandman, born Oct. 5, bapt. Nov. 2.
John s. Godfrey Newham, labourer, born Feb. 4, bapt. Feb. 12.
William s. Edward Roe, labourer, born March 12, bapt. March 21.

1708.

Ruth base d. Elizabeth Newland, born Nov. 13, bapt. Nov. 15.
Thomas s. Thomas Hyfield, born and bapt. Feb. 3.

1709.

John s. Thomas Justice, born April 4, bapt April 5.
Mary d. Samuel Story, born Dec. 14, bapt. Dec. 19.
John s. John Winterbottom & Barbara his wife, born & bapt. Feb. 15.

1710.

Thomas s. Thomas Whitlam and Anne his wife, born & bapt. April 7.
William s. Thomas Hyfield and Mary his wife, bapt. Aug. 27.
Robert s. Robert Hawkworsth, milner, born Jan. 7, bapt. Jan. 9.
William s. Wm Brunt, born & bapt. Jan. 21.

1711.

William s. John Leary & Sarah his wife, born June 15, bapt. June 28.

1712.

John s. John Dean and Anne his wife, born June 27, bapt. June 30.
William s. William Brunt and Sarah his wife, born July 10, bapt.
    July 11.
Martha d. Edward Roe, born July 5, bapt. Aug. 3.
Mary d. Thomas Hyfield, born Nov. 10, bapt. Dec. 7
William s. Thomas Whitlam and Anne his wife, born and bapt.
    Feb. 11.

1713.

John s. William Byron and Anne his wife, born and bapt. May 13.
Martha bastard d. Anne Baxter, born and bapt. Oct. 2.

1714.

Anne d. William Byron and Anne his wife, born Oct. 24. bapt. Oct. 26.
Joseph s. John Leary and Sarah his wife, born Dec. 3, bapt. Dec. 18.
William s. Luke Worsley and Mary his wife, born Jan. 14, bapt.
　　Jan. 17.
Hanna d. William Brunt and Sarah his wife, born Jan. 30, bapt.
　　Jan. 31.
Elizabeth d. Tho. Hyfield and Mary his wife, born March 8, bapt.
　　March 9.

1715.

Anne d. William Wombel and Elizabeth his wife, born May 6, bapt.
　　May 8.
Thomas s. Robt. Marshall and Elizabeth his wife, born July 10,
　　bapt. July 13.
Anne d. William Hill, Dec. 5.
John s. Samuel Story and Mary his wife, born and bapt. Dec. 13.
Anne d. John Thorpe of Haughton mill, bapt. Jan. 18.

1716.

John s. Joan Brooks of Haughton, bapt. April 17.
Mary d. William Brunt, born and bapt. Sept. 3.
William s. Wm Hill, bapt. Feb. 10.

1717.

Mary d. William and Anne Byron, born May 26, bapt. May 27.
Robert s. Robert Hather, husbandman, bapt. Nov. 21.
John s. Luke Worslay, housholder, bapt. Jan. 1.
Anne d. Thomas Hyfield, householder, bapt. Feb. 13.

1718.

Elizabeth d. William Wombell, householder, bapt. April 6.
George s. Robert Marshal, housholder, and Elizabeth his wife, bapt.
　　July 7.
Elizabeth d. Richard Ratlif, labourer, bapt. Aug. 24.
Anne d. John Brooks, householder, bapt. Sept. 14.
Allice d. John Duke, Labourer, bapt. Oct. 12.
William s. William Byron and Anne his wife, born Nov. 16, bapt.
　　Nov. 17.
Thomas s. Thomas Lee, labourer, & Mary his wife, born Jan. 31,
　　bapt. Feb. 1.
Sarah bastard d. Anne Barnes, born and bapt. Feb. 16.

1719.

William s. William Harrison, jun^r and Elizabeth his wife. Sept. 10.[1]
Elizabeth d. Robert and Elizabeth Hather. Oct. 31.
Mary d. Francis and Mary Ratlif. Jan. 31.

[1] From this time the dates are those of Baptisms only.

1720.

Mary d. hue mountain and Alice his wife. July 31.
William s. William Wombell and Elizabeth his wife.   Sept. 11.
Hannah d. Thomas hifeild and Mary his wife.   Nov. 15.
George s. Thomas Lee and Mary his wife.   March 19.

1721.

Elizabeth d. William Byrend and Anne his wife.   April 23.
Anne d. Will. Harison and Elizabeth his wife.   Sept. 23.
Tho. s. Thomas brown and Anne his wife.   Nov. 16.
Jane d. Robard Marshall and Elizabeth his wife.   Feb. 6.
Anne d. Robart Marshall and Elizabeth his wife.   Feb. 6.

1722.

William s. Richard Parkin and Mary his wife.   July 22.
Elizabeth d. hue Mountain and alice his wife.   July 22.
William s. Thomas Lee and Mary his wife.   Nov. 20.
William s. Richard Ratlife and Anne his wife.   Jan. 6.

1723.

James s. Luke Worslah and Mary his wife.   June 16.
Thomas s. John Ratlife and Elizabeth his wife.   June 17.
Lorrances s. William Wombel and Elizabeth his wife.   July 20.
Tho. s. Thomas hifeild and Mary his wife.   Aug. 14.
Tho s. William and Elizabeth Thorp.   Sept. 29.
John s. Thomas Leary and Mary his wife.   Nov. 11.
Thomas s. William Haryson and Elizabeth his wife.   March 3.

1724.

Elizabeth d. William milner and Mary his wife.   April 19.
Anne d. Rob. Hather and Elizabeth his wife.   July 19.
Sarah d. Rob. marshall.   Sept. 13.
Mary d. Richard Parkin, born Sept. 7, bapt. Oct. 4.
Dorrathy d. John Chappill and Elizabeth his wife.   Sept. 28.
William s. Will. Lopcy and Anne his wife.   Nov. 8.
John s. John Ratlife and Elizabeth his wife.   March 7.

1725.

Will. s. John Brookes and elizabeth his wife.   July 1.
Will. s. hue mountain and alice his wife.   Oct. 12.
Thomas s. Thomas Leary and mary his wife.   Nov. 14.
Sarah d. Robard Tisinton and Sarah his wife.   Jan. 3.
John s. Will. herison and Elizabeth his wife.   Feb. 20.
Elizabeth d. William Milner and Elizabeth his wife.   March 2.
John s. henry Vlyat.   March 15.
mary d. Thomas Lee and mary his wife.   March 25.

1726.

John s. William Wombel and Elizabeth his wife.   May 4.
Joseph s. Richard Ratlife and Anne his wife.   Oct. 25.
Luke s. Luke Worslah and mary his wife.   Jan. 17.
mary d. William fosterd and elizabeth his wife.   Jan. 22.

1727.

James s. Thomas Leary and Mary his wife. Jan. 14.
Robard s. Robard Tisinton and Sarah his wife. Jan. 28.
Elizabeth d. William herison. Feb. 13.
Elizabeth d. John Ratlief and Elizabeth his wife. Feb. 18.
Elizabeth d. francis Tobed [Talbot] and Mary his wife. Feb. 25.

1728.

John s. William Milner & Elizabeth his wife. May 21.
Elizabeth d. Nathanael Okeland. Jan. 21.
Jonathan Bastard s. Elizabeth Newham. March 11.

1729.

Mary d. William & Elizabeth Wombell. March 28.
Mary d. Francis & Mary Talbot. July 1.
Rich^d s. Richard & Anne Ratliffe. Jan. 11.
Francis s. Saml & Mary Clarke. Feb. 1.

1730.

Hannah d. Hugh & Alice Mountain. April 1.
Rhoda d. John Brooks of Haughton. June 3.
John s. John & Anne Bean. Aug. 7.
Elizabeth d. Nathanael Okeland. Sept. 20.

Richd Jackson, Vic^r.[1]

Elizabeth d. William & Elizabeth Foster. Oct. 8.
Mary d. John & Martha Mowson. Oct. 12.
John s. Thomas & Mary Lee. Dec. 5.
William s. William & Elizabeth Milner. Dec. 29.
William s. Thomas & Mary Leary. Jan. 16.
Richard s. John & Elizabeth Ratcliffe. Feb. 9.
Elizabeth d. Francis & Mary Talbot. March 3.

1731.

Richard s. John and Anne Bean. Nov. 26.
Hannah d. John Brooks of Haughton. Jan. 14.
William s. William & Elizabeth Milner. March 18.

1732.

Samuel s. Samuel & Mary Clarke. July 23.
Thomas s. William & Mary Harrison. Feb. 18.

1733.

Mary d. Thomas & Mary Leary. Aug. 5.
Anne d. Richard & Anne Ratliffe. Aug. 19.
Anne d. Francis & Mary Talbot. Feb. 14.

1734.

John s. John & Anne Bean. April 14.
Mary d. William and Mary Harrison. April 22.
John s. Richard & Frances Gilbert. Aug. 13.

[1] His handwriting begins in 1728.

D

Elizabeth d. John & Martha Mowson. Oct. 31.
Elizabeth d. Thomas & Elizabeth Winterbottom. Nov. 28.
Anne d. William & Elizabeth Milner. Dec. 15.
Anne d. John & Elizabeth Chappell of Haughton. Dec. 1. *(sic)*.
John s. John & Sarah Leary. Feb. 9.
Mary d. John & Elizabeth Thorpe of Haughton. Jan. 5.

1735.

John s. William & Sarah Smith. June 9.
Elizabeth d. John & Sarah Gabitas. Sept. 18.
Sarah d. Francis & Mary Talbot. Sept. 24
Ann d. Saml & Mary Clarke. Dec. 29.
Thomas s. Thomas & Mary Colley of Haughton. March 21.

1736.

Mary d. John & Anne Bean. April 8.
Benjamin s. Thomas & Mary Leary. Feb. 2.

1737.

Esther d. Francis & Mary Talbot. April 5.
Elizabeth d. William & Mary Harrison. April 24.
Francis & Richard sons of Francis & Anne Rawson. May 21.
John s. John & Elizabeth Thorpe of Haughton. Aug. 22.
Francis s. William and Sarah Smith. Oct. 20.
Henry s. Henry and Elizabeth Whitlam. Dec. 30.
Thomas s. Rob. & Anne Hay. March 24.

1738.

Sarah d. John & Sarah Gabitas. April 13.
Elizabeth d. Thomas & Anne Borebank. June 24.
Mary d. William & Mary Harrison. Sept. 3.
Anne d. John & Anne Bean. Sept. 29.
Hannah d. Francis & Mary Talbot. Oct. 6.
Mary d. Samuel & Mary Clarke. Oct. 8.
Anne d. Hugh & Jane Mountain. March 20.

1739.

Anne d. John & Elizabeth Thorpe of Haughton. Aug. 1.
John s. William & Mary Hollin. Sept. 12
Anne d. Robert & Anne Hay. Jan. 13.

1740.

Rosamond d. Francis & Mary Talbot. July 17.
William s. William Harrison, Labourer, & Mary his wife. Oct. 2
Elizabeth d. John & Sarah Gabitas. Oct. 28.

1741.

John s. Saml & Mary Clarke. Oct. 2.
Francis s. Francis & Mary Talbot. Oct. 15.
Anne d. John & Sarah Hurst. Oct. 31.
Richard s. Francis & Anne Rawson. Nov. 26.
John s. John & Sarah Gabitas. Jan. 13.
William s. John & Sarah Leary. March 22.

1742.

Hugh s. Hugh & Jane Mountain. July 2.
Mary d. Robert & Anne Hay. Aug. 1.
Joseph s. William & Mary Hollin. Dec. 29.
John s. John & Mary Moss. Feb. 17.
Thomas s. Sam¹ & Mary Clarke. Feb. 20.

1743.

John s. William & Mary Harrison. April 29.
Elizabeth d. John & Elizabeth Thorpe of Haughton. June 18.
John s. Thomas & Anne Borebank. Aug. 8.
Anne d. Wᵐ & Jane Foster. Dec. 26.

1744.

Mary d. John & Sarah Gabitas. June 13.
Anne d. William & Elizabeth Buttery. Oct. 11.
Sarah & Mary daurs. of John & Sarah Hurst. Jan. 1.
Elizabeth d. Sam¹ & Mary Clarke. Jan. 24.
Mary d. William & Mary Hollin. March 3.
John s. William & Jane Foster. March 11.

1745.

Isaac s. Robert & Anne Hay. April 18.
Mary d. John & Mary Moss. Septʳ 28.
Thomas s. John & Elizabeth Thorpe of Haughton. Oct. 16.

1746.

Jane d. William & Jane Foster. April 1.
George s. William & Mary Harrison. April 13.
Elizabeth d. William & Elizabeth Buttery. April 18.
William s. Richard & Elizabeth Harrison. Sept. 4.
Thomas s. Anne yᵉ wife of Richard Gilbert. Feb. 2.

1747.

Hannah d. John & Sarah Gabitas. June 10.
John s. William & Jane Foster. Aug. 23.
Sarah d. Sam¹ & Mary Clarke. Oct. 9.
Richard s. Richard & Anne Gilbert. Nov. 29.
Sarah d. William and Elizabeth Buttery. March 2.

1748.

Thomas s. William & Mary Harrison. June 19.
William s. Robert & Anne Hay. Nov. 18.
Elizabeth d. William & Mary Hollins. Dec. 27.
Jane d. William and Jane Foster. March 7.

1749.

Elizabeth d. John & Sarah Hurst. April 30.
Frances d. Richard & Anne Gilbert. Oct. 26.
Hannah bastard d. Hannah Holsworth. Nov. 13.

D²

1750.

Easter d. Richard & Sarah Harrison. June 13. N.B.—This child
    was born on Easter Day.
William s. William & Elizabeth Buttery. June 14.
Frances d. George & Mary Cou (? Cox).
Sarah d. John & Mary Moss. Nov. 1.
William s. Richard & Susanna Pogmore. Feb. 16.

1751.

John s. John & Mary White. June 15.
Elizabeth d. Richard & Sarah Harrison. Aug. 1.

1752.

John s. Richard & Anne Gilbert. March 1.
John s. Robert & Anne Hay. April 21.
Anne d. John & Sarah Gabitas. May 11.
Thomas s. Richard & Sarah Harrison. July 11.
Elizabeth d. Robert & Ann Tissington. Aug. 1.

1753.

Susanna d. William and Elizabeth Buttery. Jan. 12.
Francis s. Francis & Jane Talbot. Oct. 10.
Mary d. Richard & Susanna Pogmore. Oct. 25.
Mary d. Henry & Jemima Watson. Nov. 4.

1754.

John s. Jonathan & Dorothy Yates. March 3.
Elizabeth d. Mr John Hartshorn & Mary his wife. July 11.
John s. Robert & Anne Tissington. Aug. 18.
Mary d. James & Elizabeth Dunston. Aug. 19.
Sarah d. Richard & Anne Gilbert. Aug. 28.
David s. Rich^d & Sarah Harrison. Oct. 16.
William s. John & Sarah Gabitas. Oct. 24.
John s. William & Elizabeth Buttery. Dec. 17.
Mary d. Thomas & Mary Burrell. Dec. 23.

1755.

Elizabeth d. John & Sarah Walker. Feb. 23.
Mary d. William & Mary Arnold. Nov. 23.

1756.

Elizabeth d. Richard & Sarah Harrison. Jan. 19.
Thomas s. William & Elizabeth Buttery. Feb. 13.
John s. James & Elizabeth Dunston. March 27.
Mary d. Robert & Elizabeth Wilcox. April 27.
Mark s. John & Elizabeth Tissington. June 23.
Peter s. Francis & Jane Talbot. Sept. 12.
William s. Thomas & Kezia Sellers of Dority Hucknall. Sept. 29.
Anne d. Robert & Anne Tissington. Nov. 7.
John s. John & Mary Gunthorpe. Dec. 25.

1757.

Thomas s. John & Mary Jackson. Jan. 30.
Hannah d. Jonathan & Dorothy Yates. May 8.
Elizabeth d. Richard & Sarah Harrison, July 27.
William s. William & Mary Arnold. Nov. 15.

1758.

William s. Richard & Elizabeth Ratcliffe. April 3.
Mary d. John & Elizabeth Tissington. June 16.
William s. John & Mary Gunthorpe. June 18.
William natural son of Anne Darlow. July 22.
Jane d. Richard & Elizabeth Pogmore. Sept. 24.
Sarah d. Robert & Anne Tissington. Oct. 1.

1759.

Mary d. Jonathan & Dorothy Yates. Jan. 21.
Anne d. James & Elizabeth Dunston. Feb. 27.
Elizabeth d. John & Mary Moss. March 27.
Elizabeth d. John & Mary Lee. April 25.
Charles Bastard son of Mary Foster. May 3.
Martha d. Francis & Jane Talbot. June 24.
John s. William & Elizabeth Buttery. June 27.
Thomas s. John & Mary Ulyat of Haughton. July 28.
William s. Thomas & Elizabeth Strong of Haughton. Aug. 5.
Mary d. Richard & Sarah Harrison. Oct. 21.
John s. John & Mary Jackson. Dec. 7.

1760.

William s. Thomas & Mary Burrell. Feb. 27.
Samuel s. Richard & Anne Pogmore. March 9.[1]
William s. Richard & Ann Gilbert. April 13.
John s. John & Elizabeth Smith. May 1.
Thomas s. Thomas & Mary Hay of Haughton. May 10.
Mary d. John & Mary Lee. May 10.
John s. William & Mary Worseley. May 13.
Mary d. Robert & Ann Tissington. Sept. 14.
Elizabeth d. Jonathan & Dorothy Yates. Dec. 7.
Ann d. Richard & Sarah Harrison. Nov. 30.
Ann d. John & Elizabeth Dean. Dec. 14.

1761.

Mary d. John & Mary Gunthorpe. Jan. 4.
James s. James & Elizabeth Dunstan. Feb. 22.
Mary d. Richard & Ann Gilbert. March 8.
William s. Tho⁸ & Mary Hyefield. April 12.
Thomas s. Thoˢ & Elizabeth Strong of Haughton. June 28.
John s. John & Mary lee. Oct. 25.
Ann d. John & marey Chapiell. Nov. 22.
Mary d. John & Mary Jackson. Dec. 20.

[1] Last entry in Richard Jackson's hand. He was buried May 15.

1762.

Tho⁸ s. John and mary evlyat [Ulyat]. Feb. 25.
Roberd s. Roberd & ann Tisinton. March 28.
Ann d. Richard & ann pogmore. May 9.
Tho's s. Tho's and mary Hifelld. July 18.
John s. John Dean and Elizabeth Dean. Sept. 19.
Elisabath d. Tho⁸ and Elisabath Strong. Sept. 24.

1763.

Jonathan s. Jonathan & Dorety Yats. Jan. 9.
Gorge s. Tho's & Maery Hayes. Feb. 3.
Charls & Rebecah s. & d. Henery and milley Wadson. April 7.
John s. John & meary Chapell. June 26.
Joseph s. Wᵐ and Sara Hollen. June 26.
Richard s. Richard and Elisabath Ratlif. July 16.
John a bastard of An Hirst. July 18.
John s. Tho's & marey Hifelld. Nov. 20.

1764.

Gorge s. John and Elisabath Dean. Jan. 8.
Gorg s. John and marey Gonthorp. 22 Jan.
Joseph s. James & Elisabath [*blank*]. 5 Jan.
Sara d. John & Sara Jackson. 15 April.
Jonathan Cam the Son of Jonathan Cam renounced Quarerism
     [Quakerism] in this Church openly and was then Baptised
     April 29ᵗʰ in the 29ᵗʰ Year of his Age.
                              By Francis Holliday, Curate.
Richard s. John & mary vllayt [Ulyat] of hoton. 1 Aug.
Elisabath d. willam and Ann willson. 7 Oct.
Ellisabath d. Richeard and martha Rawson. Oct. 21.
Sara d. Richerd and Sara Harison. Nov. 18.
Willam s. John and Hana Wombell. Nov. 25.
Hana d. Roberd & ann Tisinton. Dec. 21.

1765.

Tho. s. Poll and Hana peason of Hoton. Feb. 25.
Richerd s. John and meary Chapell. March 2.
John s. francis Smith and An is wife. March 30.
Joesep s. Jonathan & Dorety Yotes. April 14.
Ann d. Jnᵒ & Ann Tissington. June 23.
John s. Henry & Millicent Watson. July 7.
Mary d. Tho⁸ & Mary Highfield. Dec. 30.

1766.

Jonathan s. Richᵈ & Ann Pogmore. Jan. 7.
Martha d. Willᵐ & Sarah Hollis. Feb. 6.
Michael s. Francis Brooks of Haughton, Paper-Maker. March 12.
John s. John & Ann Whitworth. March 15.
Susannah Essex d. Robᵗ & Ann Tissington. 9 April.

Willm s. John Jackson. April 13.
John s. John & Hannah Wombell. May 21.
Willm s. Jonathan & Mary Camm. July 16.
Joseph s. Dorothy Yates, Widow. July 26.
Willm s. Willm & Mary Hayton. Sept. 21.
Isaac s. John & Elizth Dean. Oct. 16.
Mary d. Rich^d & Martha Rawson. Dec. 10.
Elizth d. Robt & Ann Brown. Dec. 21.

1767.

Thomas s. Rich^d & Elizth Ratcliffe. Jan. 8.
William s. Thos & Elizth Thorpe of Haughton Mill. Feb. 8.
Elizth d. Thos & Mary Highfield. March 7.
Francis s. Francis & Ann Smith. March 14.
Dorothy d. Rich^d & Sarah Harrison. April 8.
Henry s. Henry & Millicent Watson. June 25.
Elizth d. Willm & Elizth Robinson of Haughton. July 13.
Elizth d. Jonathan & Mary Camm. July 22.
Willm s. John & Mary Chappel. Sept. 13.
Willm s. George & Mary Chapman. Oct. 13.
Elizth d. Francis Brooks. Born May 18, and Bapt. . .

1768.

Susannah d. Willm & Mary Hayton. April 7.
Henry s. Robt & Ann Tissington. April 21.
Elizth d. John & Ann Tissington. May 1.
Lawrence s. John and Hannah Wombill. June 22.
John & Willm twin sons John & Elizth Trown. Aug. 14.
Jno & Rich^d twin sons of Jno & Mary Gunthorpe. Oct. 23.
Elizth d. John & Mary Chappel. Nov. 30.
Joseph s. John & Sarah Jackson. Dec. 25.

Marm^{ke} Callis, Cur.[1]
Henry Whitlam & Saml Clarke, Churchwardens.

1769.

John s. Willm & Sarah Hollis. Jan. 2.
Willm s. Francis & ann Smith. Jan. 10.
Willm s. John & ann Whitworth. Jan. 11.
Mary d. Jonathan & Mary Camm. Feb. 3.
John s. Thomas & Elizabeth Thorpe. March 17.
Willm s. Christopher & Mary Snowden. March 17.
Ann d. Willm & Elizth Robinson of Haughton. April 13.
Will'm s. Will'm & Mary Heywood. April 23.
Thos s. Henry & Millicent Watson. Sept. 8.
Sarah d. John & Jane Revell from Edwinstow. Sept. 20.
Geo. s. Thos & Mary Highfield. Oct. 31.
John s. William & Sarah Nutt. Nov. 9.

[1] He appears to have been Curate till 1783.

1770.

Mary d. W^m & Mary Hayton. Jan. 14.
John s. Francis & Althea Brooks. Jan. 26.
John s. Robert and Ann Brown. Feb. 4.
John s. George and Mary Chapman. Feb. 5.
George s. John & Ann Tissington. March 1.
Thomas s. John & Elizth Trown. March 16.
Henry s. John & Hannah Woombill. April 8.
Martha d. Robt & Ann Tissington. April 29.
Elizth d. Rich^d & Elizth Ratcliff. July 8.
W^m s. Mary Chappel, Widow. Aug. 5.
Mathew s. Rich^d & Mary Pogmore. Aug. 30.
Sarah d. John & Ann Weightman from Mansfield. Sept. 29.
Sarah d. Thos & Sarah Lee. Oct. 22.
Elizth d. Edward & Sarah Bennett. Dec. 10.
Elizth d. Jno & Elizth Dean. Dec. 31.

1771.

Thos & George Twins sons of Francis & Ann Smith. Jan. 3.
Robt s. W^m & Mary Heywood. Jan. 7.
Francis s. Rich^d & Martha Rawson. Jan. 12.
Mary d. Thos & Mary Highfield. Jan. 28.
Willm s. Willm & Elizth Cutler. April 14.
Elizth d. Christopher & Mary Snowden. May 21.
Thos s. Thos & Elizth Thorpe. June 19.
John s. Jno & Elizth Trown. June 26.
Sarah d. Francis & Hannah Clark. June 26.
Rich^d & Thos Twins sons of Jno & Sarah Whitworth. Dec. 5.
Willm s. John & Mary Ellis. Dec. 14.

1772.

Elizth d. W^m & Sarah Mansill of Haughton. Feb. 7. about 16
    weeks old.
Elizth d. Jno & Hannah Woombill. Jan. 16.
Sarah d. Willm and Sarah Hollis. March 1.
Ann d. of George & Mary Chapman. March 13.
Jane d. Francis & Althea Brooks of Haughton. April 4.
George s. Francis & Ann Smith. June 14.
John s. John & Mary Moss. Aug. 18.
Sarah d. John & Mary Gunthorpe. Dec. 26.
Mary d. Francis & Hannah Clarke. Dec. 29.

Houghton Mill.

Willm s. Thomas & Elizth Thorpe. Born 5 Feb. 1767.
John s.   ,,   ,,   ,,   ,,   7 March 1769.
Thomas s. ,,   ,,   ,,   ,,   19 June 1771.
Willm s.   ,,   ,,   ,,   ,,   14 Oct. 1773.
Elizth d.   ,,   ,,   ,,   ,,   2 Jan. 1776.

1773.

Sarah d. William & Ann Camm. Jan. 28.
Rich^d s. Willm and Sarah Hayton. March 7.
Sarah d. & Alexander s. Will'm and Mary Heywood. April 4.
Matthew s. John and Elizth Dean. April 11.
William s. Robert & Ann Brown. June 24.
William s. William & Sarah Mansill of Haughton. Aug. 13.
Mary d. Willm & Ann Ashmore. Aug. 26.
Willm s. Tho's & Elizth Thorpe. Oct. 20.
John s. John & Sarah Gabbitass. Oct. 22.
Mary d. John & Mary Moss. Nov. 4.
Mary d. William & Mary Richards. Dec. 2.
Elizth d. John & Elizth Trown. Dec. 19.
Jane d. Christopher & Mary Snowden. Dec. 22.

1774.

Elizth d. Tho's & Elizth Mills. Feb. 15.
James s. John & Mary Ellis. Feb. 26.
Thomas s. William & Elizth Cutler. April 12.
Richard s. Francis & Ann Smith. April 15.
George s. John & Sarah Whitworth. May 27.
Mary d. John & Hannah Woombill. May 27.
Elizth d. Thos & Mary Highfield. Sept. 7.
Sarah d. John & Ann Tissington. Oct. 18.
Ann d. Rich^d & Martha Rawson. Nov. 26.
Elizth d. William & Sarah Hollis. Dec. 24.
Elizth d. Francis & Hannah Clark. Dec. 24.

1775.

George s. Geo. & Mary Chapman. Jan. 5.
John s. John & Elizth Ward. April 20.
William s. William & Ann Camm. May 1.
William s. William & Susannah Harpham. May 8.
George s. Will'm & Mary Heywood. June 22.
Sarah d. Willm & Sarah Hayton. July 19.
Newham Mary d. of Rebecca Lees base born. Aug. 25.
John s. Christopher & Mary Snowden. Sept. 3.
Thomas s. Jno & Sarah Gabbitass. Nov. 28.

1776.

Jane d. Robt & Ann Tissington. Feb. 2.
Robert s. Robt & Ann Brown. Feb. 15.
Sarah d. Willm & Sarah Mansill. Feb. 22.
Thomas s. John & Hannah Wombill. March 28.
Elizth d. John & Mary Ellis. April 7.
Samuel s. Francis & Ann Smith. May 28.
Willm s. Willm & Mary Richards. Oct. 23.
John s. John & Hannah Linnegar from Haughton. Dec. 13.

1777.

Talison d. Mary Law base born. Jan. 5.
Tho⁵ s. Thomas & Mary Ward of Haughton. Jan. 23.
Eliz^th d. Tho⁸ & Eliz^th Thorpe. Jan. 24.
John s. Rich^d & Martha Rawson. Feb. 24.
Samuel s. Francis & Hannah Clark. March 2.
Tho⁵ s. Tho⁸ & Eliz^th Spencer. June 25.
Mark s. John & Sarah Whitworth. May 21
Eliz^th d. William & Ann Camm. May 26.
Eliz^th d. Willm & Mary Buttery. June 28.

1778.

Mary d. Paul & Sarah Unwin. Jan. 13.
Willm s. John & Sarah Gabbitass. Jan. 23.
Ann d. Willm & Sarah Hayton. March 23.
Joseph s. Lazarus & Francis Watson. May 3.
Joseph s. Francis & Ann Smith. May 18.
Eleanor d. William & Mary Heywood. July 17.
John s. William & Sarah Mansill. Dec. 16.

1779.

William s. Willm & Mary Buttery. Jan. 5.
Hannah d. John & Hannah Woombill. Jan. 6.
Richard s. Robt Brown & Ann his wife. Jan. 19.
Ann d. Christ^r and Mary Snowden. Jan. 30.
Hannah d. Willm & Mary Richards. May 8.
Sarah d. John and Sarah Gabbitass. July 27.
Sarah d. Lazarus & Frances Watson. July 27.
Martha d. Rich^d & Martha Rawson. Aug. 2.
Hannah d. Francis & Hannah Clark. Sept. 5.
Mary d. William & Sarah Hollis. Sept. 7.
Jonathan s. William & Ann Camm. Nov. 20.
Sarah d. John & Sarah Whitworth. Dec. 8.
William s. John and Mary Callis. Dec. 17.[1]

1780.

Sarah d. Sarah Gray base born. Jan. 17.
William s. John & Ann Tissington. Feb. 6.
Eliz^th d. Willm and Sarah Hayton. June 15.
Mary d. Willm & Mary Buttery. Oct. 23.

1781.

Mary d. John & Eliz^th Whittaker. Jan. 2.
William s. John & Elizabeth Ward. Jan. 22.
George s. Francis & Ann Smith. Jan. 27.
Thomas s. Christopher & Mary Snowden. Feb. 4.
Henry s. John & Hannah Woombil. March 4.
Benjamin s. Joseph & Eliz^th Walker. June 18.

[1] M. Callis signs this year as " Curate.'

Susanna d. William Mansill of Haughton and Sarah his wife.   July 16.
Elizth d. Sarah Gray base born.   July 31.
Elizth d. Edmund Woodhead, Carpenter, & Ann his wife.   Aug. 1.
William s. Richd Rawson, Farmer, & Martha his wife.   Sept. 10.

1782.

Rich. s. Elizth Rawson base born.   Feb. 14.
Ann d. Robert & Ann Brown.   Feb. 22.
Ann d. Francis Clarke, Farmer & Hannah his Wife.   Feb. 24.
Ann d. John Hopkin in Haughton Lib^y Lab^r & Sarah his Wife.
　　May 28.
John s. William & Ann Camm.   July 9.
Mary d. William Heywood, Taylor, & Mary his wife.   Aug. 11.
Mary d. John Gabbitas, Farmer, & Sarah his Wife.   Aug. 23.
Sarah d. William Buttery, Farmer, & Mary his wife.   Oct. 26.
William Camm the son of Jonathan Camm renounced Quakerism in
　　this Church openly and then was baptiz'd December 27th in the
　　40th Year of his Age.

By Marm^{ke} Callis, Curate.

1783.

Francis s. Will'm & Mary Cutler Jan. 5.
Richard s. Edmund Woodg, head Carp^r, & Ann his wife.   Feb. 19.
Sarah d. Francis Smith, Grocer, & Ann his wife.   March 23.
Elizabeth d. John Whitworth, Cottager, & Sarah his wife.   March 30.
John s. Mary Harrison base born.   March 25.
Henry s. William & Sarah Mansell of Haughton.   Dec. 27.

1784.

Sarah d. John & Elizebeth Breeding of Haughton.   Aug. 8.
John s. Edmund Woodg, head Carp., & Ann his wife.   Aug. 30.
John Hurst Child was born dead.   June 7, 1701.[1]
John Winterbottom Child was born dead.   Aug. 1, 1703. *(Vide*
　　1703.)[1]
Ann d. William Camm & Ann his wife.   Sept. 5.
John s. Peter Saunderson & Sarah his wife.   Nov. 14.
Thomas s. William & Ann hollin.   Dec. 26.

1785.

Jan.	2.	Ann d. Rich^d & Eliz. Whitworth.
,,	16.	Ann d. W^m & Mary Buttry.
,,	16.	Elizabeth base born of Eliz. Cook.
Feb.	27.	Martha d. Fra^s & Hannah Clarke.
Ap.	3.	Mary d. Robt & Ann Brown.
May	21.	Richard s. Jo. & Mary Long.
,,	29.	George s. W^m & Ann Ashmore.
Ju.	26.	Thomas base born of Mary Low.

[1] Evidently written in years before 1784, it being at top of the page and in an older hand.

July 4. Mary d. Jo. & Sarah Hobkin, Haug^n.
Aug. 21. George s. Rich^d & Martha Rawson.
Sepr 11. William s. Thos and Alice Jackson.
Oct. 2. Henry s. Jo. & Alice Tissington.
Nov. 28. Mary d. Jo. & Eliz. Breedon.
Decr 18. John s. John & Mary Watkinson.

1786.

Feby 19. Lucy base born d. of Sarah Gabitas.
Ap. 18. Edmund s. Edm^d & Ann Woodhead.
Aug. 19. Charles s. George & Rebekah Hewitt.
Nov. 5. John s. Willm & Ann Camm.

1787.

Jany 5. Thomas s. Willm & Mary Buttry.
  ,,   5. John s. Willm & Ann Morfeil.
Feb. 26. Thomas s. Willm & Sarah Mansill.
Mar. 24. Ann d. Jo. & Mary Long.
  ,,   27. Francis s. Fra^s & Han^h Clark.
June 9. John s. John & Jane Dunstone.
  ,,   9. Lawrence s. John & Eliz. Ward.
  ,,   22. Nanny d. John & Eliz. Breeding, Haug^n.
Sept. 16. Sarah d. Edmund & Anne Woodhead.

1788.

William s. W^m & Ann Hollis. Feb. 17.
William s. James & Sarah Reavell. Mar. 30.
George s. Geo. & Rebekah Hewitt. May 18.
Elizabeth d. Tho's & Alice Jackson. Oct. 5.
Mary d. John & Alice Tissington. Nov. 9.

1789.

Ann d. Thomas & *Efie* White. April 2.
Rebekah d. Willm & Mary Buttry. April 12.
Mary d. Geo. & Hannah Dean. April 23.
Sarah d. W^m & Ann Camm. May 3.
Elizth d. Wm Whiteley & Eliz. Walker. May 3.
Sarah d. Geo. & Mary Gunthorp. Aug. 23.
Thomas s. William & Sarah Thornill. Oct. 9.
Richard s. Rich^d & Sarah Cook. Dec. 6.
William s. James & Sarah Reavil. Dec. 13.
John s. John & Jane Dunstone. Dec. 25.

1790.

George & Mary twins s. and d. William & Sarah Mansell. June 15.
William s. John & Anne Metham. July 25.
George s. George & Hannah Dean. Oct. 13.
Elizabeth d. George & Rebeckah Hewet. Nov. 21.

1791.

Elizabeth d. John & Ann Tomlinson. Jan. 9.
Sarah d. Richard & Elizabeth Taylor. Feb. 13.

John s. John & Elizabeth Bower. March 6.
Mary d. Thomas & Mary Watson. April 24.
Martha d. Thomas & Ann Stocks. May 22.
George s. William & Mary Buttery. June 5.
William s. Robert & Elizabeth *Holt.* June 12.
Mary d. John & Mary Long. Aug. 14.
Sarah base born of Elizabeth Walker. P. Oct. 16.

1792.

Benjamin s. Solomon & Sarah Matchett. Feb. 10.
Thomas s. John & Elizabeth Ward. March 11.
Hannah d. John & Ann Mettham. March 11.
Mary d. John & Eliz. Bower. May 27.
John s. George & Hannah Dean. July 1.
Elizabeth base born of Elizabeth Mettham, P., from Kneesal. July 1.
Joseph s. W^m & Ann Camm. Aug. 26.

A Register of all Marriages in the Parish of Walesby within the County of Nottingham. Anno Regni Regis Caroli secundi Tricessimo secundo. Annoq' Domini 1680.

William Harrison husbandman & Ann Boynby spinster. June 15, 1680.
Thomas Taylor & Elizabeth Sadler. Aug. 26, 1680.
Richard Hurst & Jane Abell. Dec. 5, 1681.
W^m son of Wm Byrand & Ann Clark daughter of Wid. Clark of Willoughby. April 25, 1682.
John Hyfield labourer & Ann Clark daughter of John Clark, Carpenter. June 29, 1682.
John Bowlsover of the Parish of Muskham & Mary Par of this Parish Wid. Jan. 30, 1682.
John Hurst & Elizabeth Regnalds. Apr. 17, 1683.
Thomas Beldam of Dunham & Hellen Patefield of Budby, wid. Oct. 2, 1863. Lic.
Jarvise Hill and Margret Byrand. April 5, 1687.
William Prestwood of this parish and Jane Nicholson of West Retford. Nov. 21, 1687.
William Parkin & Elizabeth Milner. April 28, 1689.
Richard Wright of Egmanton and Ann Clark of this parish Wid. July 2, 1689.
Richard Greenwood of Boughton & Mary Sayworth of Edwinstow. Sept. 4, 1690.
William Moss & Mary Kirkby. June 21, 1691.
Thomas Rawood & Sarah Merrils. April 23, 1693.
Henry Fox of Marnham Parish & Ann Clark of this Parish. May 2, 1693.

John Parkinson of Kirton and Barbara Arthur of Thoresby, June 22, 1693.

William Parkin & Allice Malam. July 1, 1694.

William Couper and Ann Hurst. April 4, 1695.

William Platts of Palethorp, Taylor, and Mary Dutton, dau'r of John Dutton of Haughton. Jan. 14, 1695.

John Burton of Milton in the Parish of West Markham and Hellen Whitehead of this Parish. June 29, 1696.

William Leciter, husbandman & Elizabeth Hunt, spinster, Jan. 26, 1696.

John Par, weaver and Allice Parkin, widdow. Jan. 26, 1696.

Samuel Thompson of Eakring & Mary Thorp of East Retford. May 6, 1697.

Godfrey Newham of this Parish and Ann Doncaster of Marnham parish. Nov. 11, 1697.

John Winterbottom of Welley and Barbara Howson of this parish. May 2, 1698.

John Dutton of Haughton Mill and Jane Marshall of Kirton, wid. Nov. 7, 1698.

Thomas Fielding of Palethorp and Ann Hyfield of this Parish. Oct. 15, 1700.

John Cocking of Osberton, Labourer, and Jane Dutton of East Retford spinster. Nov. 27, 1701.

William Widdows of Worksop and Jane Dutton of Walesby, spinster, Aug. 27, 1702.

James Marshal of Mansfield, Taylor, and Mary Rogers, of Walesby, spinster, Jan. 17, 1702.

Edward Roe, Labourer, and Garthurick Mitchell, spinster, Jan. 17, 1702.

William Robinson, labourer, and Elizabeth Hallywell, spinster, Jan. 23, 1703.

Thomas Wyat, Labourer, and Sarah Butcher, spinster, June 5, 1705.

Thomas Fielding of Palethorpe, Labourer, & Rebeckha Hurst of Walesby, spinster, Nov. 8, 1705.

Thomas Whitlam, husbandman, and Anne Moor, spinster, Jan. 15, 1705.

Andrew Cook of Eakring, weaver, and Sarah Thrave of Laxton, spinster, March 21, 1705.

Richard Newland of Walesby, and Elizabeth Eyre of Luxford, Aug. 8, 1708.

John Chappel of Bothamsell and Margret Hill of Walesby. Sept. 23, 1708.

Thomas Harbey of Littleborough & Mary Wyat of yᵉ Parish. April 20, 1710.

John Byron, junᵉ of Stoakham, gent. & Elizabeth d. of Wᵐ Penington, Clerk. Feb. 5, 1712.

John Woolley of Martin Parish and Elizabeth Barns of Walesby. June 24, 1713.

William Bowls of Haughton and Mary Saxalby of Boughton. May 8, 1716.

William Andrews and Elizabeth Turner both of Ollorton. July 3, 1716.

William Chambers of East Drayton & Katharine Harson of this parish, Aug. 2, 1716.

Richard Ratlif and Anne Hopkinson both of this parish, June 20, 1717. Banns.

John Duke, labourer, and Elizabeth Mussen spinster, both of Walesby, Nov. 17, 1717. Banns.

John Bean of Edwinstow, Batchelor, and Anne Whitlam of Walesby, widow, Nov. 21, 1717. Banns.

Robert Tissinton, Batchelor, and Anne Mountain, widow, both of Walesby. Feb. 6, 1717. Banns.

Luke Chappill, Batchelor, and Sarah brunt, widow, both of Walesby, Nov. 15, 1720. Banns.

William Lobcy, Batehelor and Anne Cooke, spinster, both of Walesby, Decr 8, 1720. Banns.

Richard Parkin, Batchelor, and Mary Herison, spinster, both of Walesby, April 11, 1721. Banns.

Christopher Clarke, Batchelor, and Hannah Marlah, spinster, both of Walesby. May 30, 1721. Banns.

Joseph Padlow, Widdower, of Askern, and Elizabeth Padlow, spinster of Walesby, 1 May, 1722. Banns.

William Lopcy, widdower, and anne barnes, spinster, both of Walesby, July 22, 1722, Banns.

John Bean, widdower, and Sarah Leary, widdow, both of Walesby. Oct. 2, 1722. Banns.

Will. Merrils and Elizabeth Bullard both of Walesby. Jan. 1, 1722.

Will. Milner, Batcheler, and mary michel spinster. June 4, 1723.

Rob. Tisinton, Widdower, and Sarah Smith, spinster, 1 Dec. both of Walesby, 1723.

Henry Vlyat, Batchelor and Alice Parr, spinster, both of Walesby. April 7, 1724.

John Bee of Boul, Bachelor, and Anne Parr of Walesby. April 21, 1724. Banns.

John Gabbytus of Darlton, Batchelor, and Elizabeth Hather, widow, of Walesby, Sept. 5, 1725.

Richard newland of Walesby, widower, and Elizabeth Theaker of West Draton. April 14, 1726.

Will. Fosttard, Bacheler and Elizabeth Hurst both of Walesby, April 21, 1726.

Joseph Booth and Mary Rouke. April 14, 1726.

John Firth of ollerton, Bacheler, and elinar Wombel, spinster, of Walesby. May 7, 1727.

William Hill & Esther Pickering. April 8, 1729.

Francis Cutts & Grace Wild both of this Parish. April 6, 1730.

John Allen & Barbara Thorpe, both of Wellow, May 12, 1730.

Joseph Snowden & Mary Beckett both of Wellow. Aug. 30, 1730.

Edward Lee of Clipston & Sarah Tiers of this Parish, Nov. 12, 1730.

David Graves of Laxton & Elizabeth Hind of Wellow. Decr 26, 1730.

John Leary & Sarah Scoles both of this Parish. Feb. 22, 1730.

1731.

Jonathan Bradley of Elksley & Dorothy Slack of this Parish. May 13. Licence.

Robt Hunt of Bothomsall & Elizabeth Thorpe of Haughton in this Parish, June 7, Banns.

1732.

Theophilus Rodgers & Elizabeth Ginnover both of Wellow. April 11. Banns.

William Harrison & Mary Reynolds both of this Parish. April 16. Banns.

John Ward of Ossington & Martha Mason of Retford. Nov. 9. Licence.

Robert Gilbert of Wellow & Cassandra Peace of Ordsall. Nov. 30. Banns.

1733.

William Baker of Caunton & Sarah Winterbottom of this Parish. April 19. Banns.

Thomas Stronge of this Parish & Anne Smith of Wellow. July 10. Banns.

Richard Gilbert & Frances Hurst both of this Parish. Aug. 2. Banns.

Thomas Winterbottom of this Parish & Elizabeth Robinson of Bothomsall. Jan. 24. Banns.

John Winterbottom of this Parish & Eliz. Smith of West Markham. Feb. 24. Banns.

1734.

William Smith & Sarah Marshall both of this Parish. June 30. Banns.

Thomas Colley & Mary Brookes both of Haughton in this Parish. Jan. 5. Banns.

John Wadson of Kirsall & Margaret Leavers of Wellow. Jan. 6. Banns.

Joseph Worsley & Jane Lill both of Haughton in this Parish. Jan. 12. Banns.

John Pearson of this Parish & Elizabeth Merill of Lutton sup^r Lound. Feb. 11. Banns.

1735.

John Priest & Alice Dalton both of this Parish. May 6. Banns.

John Gamble of Worksop & Mary West of Tuxford. May. 8. Licence.

John Cooke & Elizabeth Rag both of this Parish. Oct. 16. Banns.

1736.

Robert Hunt of East Drayton & Elizabeth Marshall of this Parish. April 29. Banns.

Richard Cogil & Mary Whitworth both of Wellow. June 8. Banns.

Edward Blyton of Kneesall & Mary Marshall of Wellow. June 20. Banns.

William Harrison & Mary Hurst both of this Parish. July 15. Banns.

Charles Cogill & Mary Turner both of Wellow. Nov. 15. Banns.

Joshuah Lawrence of Bottomsall & Anne Bettison of this parish.
Dec. 2. Banns.

William Leary of this Parish & Anne Salmon of Ollerton. Dec. 7.
Banns.

Jonathan Clarke of Rufford & Anne Whitworth of Wellow. Jan. 20.
Banns.

Robert Hay & Anne Jenkinson both of this Parish. Jan. 25. Banns.

1737.

Hugh Mountain & Jane Newland both of this Parish. April 11.
Banns.

Benjamin Roberts of Ollerton & Mary Peatfield of Wellow. April 12.
Licence.

John Bett & Sarah Powell both of Wellow. June 20. Banns.

William Bacon of Wellow & Hannah Russel of Rufford. Dec. 21.
Banns.

1739.

William Blyton & Anne Dean both of Wellow. June 12. Banns.

Joseph Pounder & Mary Handley both of Wellow. Sept. 18. Banns.

William Peatfield of Budby & Anne Bean of this Parish. Oct. 22.
Banns.

John Gilbert of Kirkton & Mary Hyefield of this Parish. Jan. 24.
Banns.

1740.

William Worseley & Elizabeth Fairclouff both of this Parish. Aug. 14.
Banns.

1742.

William Foster & Jane Hopkinson both of this Parish. Feb. 9.
Banns.

1743.

Thomas Lee & Anne Wombell both of this Parish. April 19.
Banns.

1745.

William Renton of Barwick in Elmet & Sarah Batty of Wellow.
June 2. Banns.

Thomas Dennis & Elizabeth Raworth both of Wellow. Sept. 22.
Banns.

George Rich & Anne Taylor both of Tuxford. Sept. 26. Banns.

1746.

John Harpham & Rebecca Ashford both of this Parish. March 31.
Banns.

William Lee & Martha Pickering both of this Parish. Aug. 12.
Banns.

Richard Gilbert & Anne Brett both of this Parish. Aug. 14. Banns.

John Raines & Elizabeth Bottomly both of Tuxford. Aug. 18. Banns.

1748.

Robert Merrins & Mary Lawrence both of this Parish. Nov. 10.
Banns.

E

1749.

Robert Marshall of this Parish & Anne Fletcher of Edwinstow. May 15. Banns.

Mr Matthew Markland of Egmanton & Mrs Mary Chappel of this Parish. June 5. Licence.

Richard Harrison of this Parish & Sarah Laws of Boughton. July 24. Banns.

Mr Thomas Harris of Thoresby & Mrs Mary Sellers of Tuxford. Aug. 18. Licence.

Thomas Wells of Norwell & Mary Gray of Wellow. Oct. 9. Banns.

John Berkin of Ollerton & Mary Smith of Wellow. Oct. 31. Licence.

William Harrison & Elizabeth Moor both of this Parish. Nov. 14. Banns.

1750.

John White & Mary Lee both of this Parish. April 17. Banns.

Robert Smith of Wellow, & Elizabeth Lawrence of Bottomsall. Aug. 28. Banns.

Thomas Bomford & Anne Revel both of Wellow. Nov. 20. Banns.

1751.

Robert Tissington & Anne Thompson both of this Parish. Nov. 13. Banns.

1752.

John Troown & Elizabeth Milner both of this Parish. Jan. 21. Banns.

Robert Smith & Dorothy Stones both of Wellow. Aug. 20. Banns.

Henry Watson of Haughton & Jemima James of this Parish. Dec. 24. Licence.

1753.

Richard Booth of Mattersey & Mary Housley of this Parish. July 19. Banns.

John Martin & Mary Bennett both of Wellow. Aug. 9. Banns.

Robert Hay & Sarah Leary both of this Parish. Aug. 21. Banns.

James Dunston & Elizabeth Rawson both of this Parish. Sept. 3. Banns.

Job Surgey of Wellow & Mary Johnson of Rufford. Oct. 7. Banns.

A Register of all Burials in the Parish of Walesby within the County of Nottingham. Anno Regni Regis Caroli secundi Tricessimo secundo Annoq' Domini 1680.

John Hurst, husbandman. June 4.

William Par, Labourer. Oct. 12.

Grace Hathar, Wid. Oct. 28.

John Worselay, husbandman. Dec. 29.

Jane Par, wid. Jan. 3.

1681.

James Cam. sen. husbandman. April 3.
William s. Wm Hurst. April 22.
Thomas s. Wm Hyfield. June 2.
Allice Flintham, wid. June 16.
Elizabeth Cam, wid. Oct. 5.
Mary d. Robt & Ann Parkinson. Oct. 30.
Elizabeth wife of Hen. Whitlam. Oct. 31.
John Par, husbandman, Nov. 13.
Dorothy Wyat, wid. Nov. 21.
Ann d. Wid. Newham. Nov. 25.
Thomas Stoakes, jun^r husbandman. Dec. 6.
Ann d. Charles & Catherine Warrener. Dec. 30.
Richard Mountaine, Labourer. March 21.
Elizabeth wife of John Hyfield. March 22.

1682.

Dorothy wife of James Freeborrow. April 6.
Richard s. W^m & Mary Hyfield. April 15.
Richard s. Thomas Taylor. Oct. 20.
Marjary Hurst, spinster. Jan. 5.
Mary wife of James Cam. Feb. 4.
Mary d. Robt & Ann Parkinson. Feb. 5.

1683.

Nathan s. Fran. & Margret Johnson. June 4.
Elizabeth wife of Hen. Whitlam. June 15.
Richard Scot, Labourer. June 17.
Hen. s. Godfrey & Ann Newham. June 18.
Thomas Taylor, Labourer. Nov. 11.
Elizabeth Scot, Wid. Jan. 20.
Elizabeth d. Wm Cook. Feb. 21.

1684.

Ann Johnson, Wid. Nov. 2.
Cuthbert s. John & Jane Bacon. Jan. 12.
William Byrand, husbandman. Feb. 3.
William s. W^m & Mary Hyfield. Feb. 2 .
Margret wife of Fran. Johnson. March 15.
William s. Godfrey & Ann Newham. March 15.

1685.

Robert s. John & Ann Clark. May 2.
Robert Parkinson, husbandman. June 29.
Ann d. Rich. & Isabell Milnes. July 7.
John Clark, Carpenter. Nov. 29.
Charles Warrener, Labourer. Dec. 19.
John s. W^m & Ann Harrison. Dec. 22.
  E²

1686.

Ann d. John & Elizabeth Hurst. April 9.
Elizabeth d. John & Ann Hyfield. Feb. 8.
Mary Clark of Willoughby, wid. Feb. 20.

1687.

Hellen wife of Thomas Mitchel. June 8.
Robert s. Wid. Wombel. June 26.
John s. Henry & Rosamond Whitlam. Jan. 9.
Elizabeth Hyfield, wid. March 7.
John s. Elizabeth Taylor, wid. March 20.

1688.

Thomas Stoakes, senex. Oct. 17.

1689.

Ann Cook. June 26.
Bridgit Rawson, Wid. July 10.
James Cook, Labourer. Aug. 4.
Henry s. Henry Whitlam. Nov. 28.
Elizabeth d. W^m & Jane Prestwood. Dec. 29.
Ann wife of William Cook. Jan. 23.

1690.

John s. W^m & Ahn Harrison. April 18.
Elizabeth wife of Will'm Moss. June 25.
Thomas s. Hanna Stoakes. Oct. 16.
Mary d. William Moss. Dec. 9.
Richard Wright, Labourer. Dec. 26.
Jane d. Wm Cook. Jan. 6.
Elizabeth d. Ann Wright. Feb, 2.

1691.

Barbara wife of Chr. Mountain. May 17.

1692.

Henry s. Henry & Elizabeth Stoaks. May 23.
Susana d. Godfrey Newham. Oct. 19.

1693.

Elizabeth wife of Will'm Parkin. April 14.
Elizabeth d. Will'm Parkin. May 8.
Elizabeth wife of Will'm Hurst. June 11.
Ann d. Thomas Mitchel. June 14.
Thomas s. William Parkin. July 19.
Ruth Howson, wid. Oct. 5.
Richard s, William Hurst. Nov. 24.
Mary Harrison, Virgo. Dec. 13.

1694.

Elizabeth Scot. April 26.
William Cook, Labourer. July 25.

1695.

Philip s. Thomas & Susanna Mountain. July 16.
Richard s. William & Ann Harrison. Sept. 12.
Hellen wife of William Lecitor. Jan. 15.

1696.

Henry s. Thomas Stoakes late of Walesby. April 15.
William Parkin, Weever. April 21.
William s. Thomas Mitchel. May 28.
Ann wife of Godfrey Newham. July 1.
Sarah Wynfield, spinster. July 19.
John Bacon, husbandman. Aug. 7.
. . . d. Richard Mills. Aug. 31.

1697.

Martha d. Christopher Clark and Mary his wife. July 17.
Anne wife of Wm Prestwood. Oct. 11.
Jane d. Thomas Wyat and Catherine his wife. Nov. 14.
William Hurst, Labourer. Jan. 25.
Ann d. Thomas Justice. Feb. 21.

1698.

Francis Butler, Labour^r. Oct. 30.
Thomas Mitchell, labourer. March 10.
John Hyfield, labourer. March 11.

1699.

John s. Jarvise Hill & Margret his wife. April 6.
Jane d. Thomas Wyat. April 14.
Elizabeth d. Tho. Wyat. April 14.
Susaña wife of Tho. Mountain. July 4.
Jane Bacon, wid. July 27.
Elizabeth d. Thomas & Ann Justice. Dec. 8.
John s. Christopher and Mary Clark. Jan. 4.
Mary d. Wm Pennington, Clerk, & Mary his wife died Jan. 28,
   buried Jan. 29.

1700.

Francis s. Richard Bean. Feb. 18.
William Lecitor Labourer. March 7.

1701.

Robert s. John Par. April 11.
Mary d. Elizibeth Lecitor, wid. April 28.
Frances Newham, wid. Dec. 29.
William s. Christopher Clark and Mary his wife. Feb. 14.

1702.

Allice Merills. Oct. 7.

1703.

William s. John Winterbottom. Aug. 4.
John s. John Winterbottom. Aug. 8.

Rebekah *Scatcherd*.   Jan. 14.
Elizabeth d. Thomas Wyat.   March 10.
John Hurst, jun[r].   March 16.

1704.

Anne d. John Hurst.   March 29.
Katherine wife of Thomas Wyat.   April 20.

1705.

George s. Robert Daft, Labourer.   May 4.
Anne d. Edward Ree, Labourer.   June 6.
Joseph s. Christopher Clark, husbandman.   Aug. 20.
Sarah d. Thomas Justice, Labourer.   Dec. 6.

1706.

Anne wife of Elias Hyfield, Labourer.   April 16.
Elias Hyfield, Labourer.   June 11.
George s. Samuel Story, Labourer.   Sept. 7.
Gervase Hill, Labourer.   Jan. 18.

1707.

James Freberrow, yeoman.   June 5.
Luke s. Tho. Mountain, Labourer.   July 19.
Anne wife of Godfrey Newham.   Feb. 12.
John s. Godfrey Newham.   Feb. 22.
Richard Aton, Labourer.   Feb. 28.
Mary wife of W[m] Moss, Labourer.   March 4.
William Prestwood, Yeoman.   March 16.
William Moss, Labourer.   March 18.
Elizabeth wife of Rich : Newland, lab[r].   March 21.

1708.

Mary wife of W[m] Hyfield.   April 8.
Elizabeth Taylor, wid.   Nov. 5.
Mary wife of Sam. Story.   Nov. 7.
Christopher Clark, husbandman.   Nov. 12.
Mary Clark, wid.   Nov. 16.
Thomas s. Tho. Hyfield.   Feb. 7.

1709.

John Winterbotton, labourer.   Dec. 29.
Godfrey Newham, labourer.   Feb. 1.

1710.

William s. Edward Roe.   Feb. 10.

1711.

John Clark.   April 17.
William s. William Brunt.   July 31.

1712.

Elizabeth Wombell.   April 4.
Lawrence Wombell, labourer.   May 11.
Mary wife of W[m] Pennington, Clerk.   May 21.
William Upton, husbandman.   Nov. 18.

1713.

Richard Bean, Labourer. March 31.
Mary d. Sam. Story. April 9.
John s. William Byron. May 15.

1714.

Christopher Mountain, senex. April 26.
Henry Whitlam, husbandman. Sept. 9.
Sarah d. Charles Harson. Oct. 5.

1716.

Isabel wife of Richard Mills. April 8.
Willliam Bradlay of Haughton, labourer. May 18.
Anne d. Richard Mills. Dec. 6.
John s. Sam. Story. Feb. 2.

1717.

James Freeborrow, yeoman. June 2.
Francis Freborrow. June 18.
Mary d. William Byron, Yeoman. Oct. 11.
Thomas s. Thomas Justice, Labourer. Dec. 15.
William Hurst, Batchelor. Jan. 12.

1718.

William Cook, Batchelor. Nov. 16.
William Brunt, husbandman. Dec. 7.

1719.

Richard Mills, Labourer. July 19.
Anne d. John Byron. Aug. 23.
Edward Roe, labourer. Oct. 20.
Anne Hather, spinster. Jan. 22.

1720.

Sarah wife of Thomas Rawood, husbandman. April 22.
William Pennington, Clerke. May 25. Who was 41 yeares Vicar
   of this Parrish.
Garick Rooe, Widdow. March 12.

1721.

Hannah d. Thomas Hifeld. May 8.
Thomas Watson, a poor man. Sept. 10. a traviler.
Isabel Hather, spinster. Sept. 30.
Sarah barnes. Nov. 10. ye child of anne barnes.
Anne wife of William Lopcy. Dec. 6.
Will. Harison, husbandman. Dec. 23.
John Learey, husbandman. Jan. 12.

1722.

Tho. Rawood, husbandman. April 6.
Tho's Mountain, Labour. Oct. 2.
John s. Christopher Clarke. Jan. 16.

1723.

Anne wife of Robard Tissiton, Labourar. May 29.
Tho. s. hue mountain, Labourar, Aug. 23.

1724.

Richard Ratlife, Labourer. March 30. poor.
Mary wife of William miller, Labourer. April 27.
Rob. Hather, husbandman. April 28.
Elizabeth d. William Milner. May 4.
Anne d. Elizabeth hather. July 20.
William Byrend, husbandman. Jan. 17.
Elizabeth wife of John Ratlife, Labourer. March 7.
Charls harson, Labour. March 16.

1725.

John Clark, Bachelor. April 29.
Elizabeth wife of Richard Newland, Labourer. Sept. 26.
Samuel s. Christophor Parke. Feb. 20.

1726.

barbarra Ratlife. Dec. 10.

1727.

Mary d. William fostord. March 31.
Jane Stokes, Widdow. May 15. 1727.
Ann Byrend, Widdow. Oct. 3.
John s. henry Vlyat Oct. 25.
John Dean, husbandman. Oct. 26.
Anne herison, Widdow. Oct. 28.
Sarah the Wife of Robard Tisinton. Jan. 28.
Mary Bean, Widdow. Feb. 18.

1728.

mary marshall d. Robard marshall. March 31.
Robard Tisinton, Labourer. April 4.
Thomas Hyfield. May 6.
Elizabeth w. Wm Harrison. June 25.
John s. Henry Ulyeat of Boughton. Aug. 9.
Elizabeth d. Francis & Mary Talbot. Aug. 18.
Elizabeth d. Wm Harrison. Aug. 26.
Sarah d. Richd Newland. Oct. 13.
Mary w. Luke Worseley. Nov. 12.
Elizabeth d. John & Elizabeth Ratcliff. Nov. 29.
Margaret w. John Marshall. Dec. 27.
Elizabeth w. John Kitchin of Budby. Jan. 23.
Elizabeth Newham. March 11.

1729.

Jonathan bastard s. Elizabeth Newham. March 25.
Elizabeth w. John Hurst. March 27.
Sarah w. John Bean. May 26.
Joseph Leary. June 27.

Luke s. Luke Worseley. July 25.
William s. Hugh Mountain & Alice his w. Aug. 14.
Elizabeth d. Nathanael Akeland. Aug. 29.
John s. Luke Worsley. Dec. 12.
Thomas s. Wm Harrison. Dec. 27.
Edward Haywood. March 9.

1730.

John s. John & Anne Bean. Aug. 18.
Alice w. Hugh Mountain. Dec. 3.
Luke Worsley. Dec. 10.
Hannah d. Hugh Mountain. Dec. 22.
William s. W^m & Elizabeth Milner. Jan. 8.
Robert Marshall. Feb. 7.

1731.

Mary w. Thomas Bell of Boughton. Feb. 1.
James s. Thomas & Mary Leary. March 6.

1732.

Ignotus a male child found in the Parish of Palethorpe. Mar. 31.
Wm Byron of Bevercotes. Nov. 17.
Richard s. Richard & Anne Ratliffe. Jan. 31.
Thomas Hurst. Feb. 18.

1733.

Elizabeth d. Richard & Anne Ratliffe. July 16.
William s. William & Eliz. Milner. Nov. 23.
Henry s. Henry & Alice Ulyeat of Boughton. Feb. 25.
Hannah w. Christopher Clarke of Budby. March 7.

1734.

Ellin w. Nath. Okeland. July 14.
William Milner. July 17.
John s. Richard & Frances Gilbert. Sept. 4.
Anne d. William & Elizabeth Milner. Dec. 16.

1735.

John s. William & Sarah Smith. June 10.
Elizabeth d. John & Sarah Gabitas. Nov. 6.
John Mowson. Jan. 13.
John s. Henry & Alice Ulyeat of Boughton. Jan. 14.
John s. John & Anne Bean. Mar. 14.

1736.

Thomas Wyat. June 7.
John s. John & Sarah Gabitas. Nov. 18.
Mary d. Christopher Clarke of Budby. Jan. 20.
Anne d. Elizabeth Fareclouf. Feb. 22.

1737.

Richard s. Francis & Anne Rawson. June 7.
Elizabeth d. William & Mary Harrison. Aug. 12.
Margaret w. Benj. Bean. Nov. 10.

Elizabeth w. Henry Whitlam.   Dec. 30.
Esther d. Francis & Mary Talbot.   Feb. 1.

1738.

Thomas Ward an Infant.   May 9.
John Bean.   Nov. 21.
John Hurst.   Feb. 14.

1739.

Richard Newland.   March 6.

1740.

Elizabeth d. Thomas & Anne Borebank.   March 22.
Barbara Winterbottom.   Nov. 4.
John Winterbottom.   Feb. 3.
Joseph s. Rich^d & Anne Ratcliffe.   March 13.

1741.

Anne Bean an Infant.   June 11.
Mrs Woodcock, Widow.   July 9.
Anne d. Robt & Anne Hay.   Sept. 17.
Alice w. John Parr.   Sept. 26.
Mary w. Francis Talbot.   Oct. 15.
Elizabeth Worseley, Widow.   Oct. 10.
John s. Saml & Mary Clarke.   Oct. 22.
Elizabeth w. William Foster.   Nov. 14.
Thomas s. John Ratcliffe.   Jan. 8.

1742.

Anne d. Thomas & Eliz. Cutler.   June 5.
Christopher Clarke of Budby.   Sept. 6.
Anne d. Mary Hyefield.   Sept. 20.
Anne w. Wm Foster.   Dec. 6.
Francis s. Francis Talbot.   Jan. 10.
Thomas s. Samuel & Mary Clarke.   Feb. 24.

1743.

Thomas Winterbottom.   July 26.
Sarah Wyat, Widow.   Feb. 8.

1744.

Francis s. Francis & Anne Rawson.   June 1.
Frances w. Richard Gilbert.   Oct. 7.
John Leary.   Feb. 18.
Mary d. John & Sarah Hurst.   Feb. 22.
John s. William & Jane Foster.   March 13.

1746.

Richard Ratcliffe.   April 16.
Thomas Harrison.   May 4.
Jane d. W^m & Jane Foster.   July 3.
Elizabeth w. Richard Harrison.   Sept. 4.
Anne Ratcliffe, Widow.   Jan. 11.
Thomas Justice.   Jan. 17.

1747.

William s. Richard Harrison.   July 27.
Samuel Clarke.   Oct. 25.
John s. William & Jane Foster.   Nov. 8.

1748.

Elizabeth Marshall, Widow.   April 26.
Anne Justice, Widow.   Nov. 26.
Elizabeth w. Richard Jackson, Vic^r.   Feb. 1.

1749.

William Harrison, Labourer.   Oct. 18.
Hannah Bastard d. Hannah Halsworth.   Nov. 27.

1751.

John Marshall.   May 24.
Elizabeth d. Richard & Sarah Harrison.   Aug. 2.

1752.

Luke Chappell.   May 26.
Thomas s. Richard & Sarah Harrison.   July 12.
John Leary.   Nov. 9.

1753.

John Parr.   Jan. 9.
Anne w. Robt Hay.   Feb. 13.
John s. Robert Hay.   April 7.
Sarah w. John Jepson of Worksop.   May 5.
Anne w. John Dean.   June 28.

1754.

Elizabeth Hose an Infant.   May 25.
Jane w. Hugh Mountain.   Nov. 27.
John s. W^m & Eliz. Buttery.   Dec. 26.

1755.

Elizabeth Winterbottom of Bevercotts, Widow.   Feb. 16.
Elizabeth d. John & Sarah Walker.   Feb. 26.
Jemima w. Henry Watson.   July 20.
Richd Bean.   Aug. 11.
Sarah d. Richard & Anne Gilbert.   Sept. 6.

1756.

Elizabeth d. Richard & Sarah Harrison.   Feb. 5.
Susanna w. Richard Pogmore.   Feb. 7.
Samuel Story.   June 3.
Sarah Leary.   Dec. 4.

1757.

Lawrence Wombell.   Jan. 27.
Jane Marshall.   Feb. 9.
John s. John & Mary Gunthorpe.   March 2.
Elizabeth w. William Worseley.   April 5.
Peter s. Francis & Jane Talbot.   June 6.
Sarah d. Thomas Hurt of Sheffield.   Sept. 12.

1758.

Sarah Chappell, Widow.   Jan. 19.
William Wombell.   May 9.
Mary w. Thomas Lee.   May 13.
Elizabeth w. Richard Pogmore.   Sept. 24.
Dorothy w. Benjn Bean.   Oct. 2.
Sarah w. Robert Hay.   Nov. 5
Thomas s. John Parkin of Boughton.   Dec. 21.
Anne w. Thomas Lee of Truswell.   Dec. 25.

1759.

John Gabitas, a minor.   Feb. 12.
Charles Bastard s. Mary Foster.   May 6.
John s. Jonathan Yates.   June 20.
John s. William Buttery.   July 12.
Mary d. Richard Harrison.   Dec. 3.
Mary Story, Widow.   Dec. 9.

1760.

William s. Richard Pogmore.   March 9.
John Parkin of Boughton.   May 2.
Richd Jackson, Clerk, May 15, who was 40 years Vicar of this Parish.

1761.

An w. John Marshall.   Sept. 11.
Mary d. Richerd and an Gillberd.   Oct. 1.
Caster s. John maskieu.[1]   Oct. 26.

1762.

Mary d. John and mary Jackson.   Feb. 10.
Widow Hifilld.   March 22.

1763.

Marcy w. John Jackson.   Feb. 7.
Roberd marshall.   July 24.
Widow Harpem.   Aug. 15.
Daved s. Richard & Sara Harrison.   Nov. 21.
Willam Hollin.   Dec. 29.
Elesabeth w. John Tisinton.   Dec. 30.

1764.

John s. an Hirst.   Jan. 2.
Sara w. Willam Smith.   Dec. 10.

1765.

John Revell.   March 9.
Joseph s. Jonathan and Dorothy Yeats.   April 21.
Josep s. Jams and Ellisabath Donston.   May 26.
Tho's Lee.   July 7.
John s. Sara *Daran*.   Aug. 11.
Willm Worsley, Taylor.   Dec. 11.
John Ratcliff.   Dec. 20.
Elizabeth w. John Ratcliffe.   Dec. 31.

---

[1] ? Mastien. The writing is that of a very illiterate person.

1766.

Mary d. Thomas & mary Highfield. Jan. 2.
Elizabeth w. James Dunstan. Jan. 9.
Sarah w. John Hurst. Jan. 11.
Elizabeth w. John Troown. Jan. 15.
John Fletcher. Jan. 19.
James s. Willm Leary. Jan. 23.
Ann w. Richd Pogmore. Jan. 30.
James Dunstan, Wid^{wr}. Feb. 2.
Jonathan s. Richd Pogmore. Feb. 5.
Mary w. John Moss. Feb. 20.
Elizth w. Willm Buttery. Feb. 25.
Sarah d. Richard Harrison. March 14.
Jonathan Yates, Blacksmith. April 16.
John s. Henry & Millicent Watson. Sept. 9.
Willm s. Jonathan Camm. July 24.
Martha Ratcliffe. Nov. 17.
Benjn Bean, Widower. Dec. 29.

1767.

Ann Dean, Widow. Jan. 1.
Ann Dunstan a poor Orphan. March 26.
Willm Harrison, Farm^r. June 3.
Willm s. John & Mary Chappell. Sept. 25.

1768.

William s. John & Elizth Trown. Aug 16.
John s. John & Elizth Trown. Sept. 15.
Ann w. Wm Peatfield, Farmer. Oct. 23.
Elizth d. John & Mary Chappell. Dec. 11.

1769.

Thomas Cutler. May 2.
Mr Francis Chappell, Batchelor. Sept. 28.
George s. Thos & Mary Highfield. Dec. 8.
Ann w. John Whitworth. Dec. 25.

1770.

John Chappell, Farmer. Feb. 13.
Thos s. John & Elizth Trown. April 29.
W^m s. Mary Chappell, widow. Aug. 15.
Sarah w. Thos Lee. Oct. 22.

1771.

Geo. s. John & Ann Tissington. Jan. 5.
Francis Talbot. Feb. 1.
Willm s. Thos & Mary Highfield. March 21.
Elizth d. Tho's and Mary Highfield. March 25.
Willm Smith. April 15.
Elizth Woombill, Widow. April 20.
Geo. s. Francis & Ann Smith. June 21.

1772.

Henry s. John & Elizth Woombill.   March 17.
Nathaniel Okeland.   July 18.

1773.

Sarah d. William & Ann Camm.   Jan 28.
Sarah w. William Woofitt.   March 30.
George son Francis & Ann Smith.   July 13.
Rich^d s. Will'm & Sarah Hayton.   July 24.
Mary d. William & Ann Ashmore.   Sept. 10.
Richd Gilbert.   Nov. 5.

1774.

William Harrison, Senior.   April 6.

1775.

Mary w. John Moss.   March 31.
Elizth w. Will'm Highfield.   April 26.
Thomas Marshall from Knapthorpe.   April 29.
Francis Rawson, Farmer.   Aug. 17.

1776.

John Hollis.   June 29.
Jonathan s. Jn° Bartrop of Ollerton.   June 29.
William s. William & Susannah Harpham.   July 10.
William s. W^m & Mary Richards.   Dec. 16.

1777.

Mary Clarke, Widow.   March 2.
Sarah Gabbitass, Widow.   Dec. 10.

1778.

William s. John Gabbitass & Sarah his wife.   Feb. 12.
Ann d. Robert & Ann Tissington.   May 23.
Elizth d. William & Ann Camm.   Oct. 29.
Thos Spencer.   Nov. 23.

1780.

Robert s. William & Mary Heywood.   Feb. 26.
Mary d. John & Hannah Woombill.   March 6.
William Peatfield.   June 17.
Mary w. Thomas Leary.   Sept. 29.

1781.

Mary w. Christopher Snowden.   May 9.
John s. John Jackson Lab^r.   May 19.
Thomas Highfield, Cottager.   Aug. 3.
Thomas Leary (late Clark).   Oct. 3.
Thomas s. Christ^r Snowden, Clark.   Oct. 21.
John s. Mary Tissington.   Dec. 9.
William Hayton, Paper Maker.   Dec. 27.

1782.

Elizabeth d. Sarah Gray.   Jan. 14.
Hanna w. John Woombill, Farmer.   March 26.

Sarah d. William & Sarah Hollin. April 4.
Elizth d. W^m & Sarah Hollin. May 8.
John Dean, Farmer. Oct. 26.
Robert Hay. Dec. 17.

1783.

Sarah d. Francis Smith, Grocer, & Ann his wife. June 22.
John s. William Camm, Carp^r & Ann his [wife] July 24.
William Parkin a Servt to George Marshall. Aug. 9.
Dorothy w. John Watkinson, Labourer. Sept. 4.
Sarah d. Lazarus d. Frances Watson. Sept. 10.
Piping John from Lincoln. P.¹ Oct. 23.

1784.

Elizabeth d. John & Sarah Whitworth. Jan. 18.
Thomas Brealey, P. widower, from Ollerton. Jan. 24.
John Gabitas, farmer. April 6.

1785.

July   11.   John Trown.
Aug.   11.   Ann Rawson.

1786.

March   13.   Sarah w. Willm Hollis.
April   12.   Sarah w. Richd Harrison.
July   30.   Richard Harrison.
Sept.   9.   William Leary.
Oct.   28.   Mary Hollis.
Nov.   10.   John Parr.

1787.

Nov.   26.   Sarah Reavell, wid^w.

1788.

April   3.   John Hurst. P.
,,   4.   Mary w. Richard Cook.
Nov.   10.   Ann Hurst. P.

1789.

Feb.   11.   William s. James & Sarah Reavell.
Mar.   1.   John s. John & Jane Dunston.

1790.

July   3.   William s. James & Sarah Reavel.

1791.

Jan.   13.   Mary d. Benjⁿ & Ann Leiary.
April   10.   John Tissington. P.
,,   21.   William s. John & Ann Mettham.
Aug.   26.   Elizabeth Cutler P. Widow.

---

¹ P=Poor.

INDEX LOCORUM.

Compiled by Sidney J. Madge, F.R.S.L.

[An asterisk (*) signifies that the place or name occurs more than once on the page.]

INDEX NOMINUM.

Compiled by SIDNEY J. MADGE, F.R.S.L.

[Irregularities.— . . . Abra., 18 ; . . . Ampllates, 20; . . . Barb., 3; . . . Bridg., 15; . . . Eliz., 4, 38 ; . . . Jas., 38 ; . . . Jn., 16 ; . . . Jos., 38 ; . . . Jud., 18 ; . . . Lawr., 4 ; . . . My., 4, 16 ; Hy . . ., Alice, 15 ; Ignotus, a male child found in the Parish of Palethorpe, 57].

Gilbert, Ann, 35*, 36*, 37*, 49, 59;
 Cassandra, 48; Frances, 33, 35, 48,
 57, 58; Jn., 33, 36, 49, 57; My., 37,
 49; Ric., 33, 35*, 36*, 37*, 48, 49,
 57, 58, 59, 62; Rob., 48; Sar., 36, 59;
 Thos., 35; Wm., 37
Gillberd, Ann, 60; My., 60; Ric., 60
Ginnover, Eliz., 48
Gliforth, Joel, 6; Rog., 6
Glined, Eliz., 3
Goeforth, Ann, 14; Ric., 14
Goforth, Ric., 12*
Goforts, Ann, 3; Ric., 3
Gonthorp, Geo., 38; Jn., 38; My., 38
Gosforth, Ric., 11*
Gouldsberie, Marg., 3; Ric., 3
Graves, Dav., 47; Eliz., 47
Gray, Eliz., 43, 62; My., 50; Sar., 42*,
 43, 62
Gredgary, Jn., 18*, 19; My., 19
Gredgrie, Jn., 18
Greene, Alice, 4; Edmid, 4
Greenwood, My., 45; Ric., 45
Greey, —, 19; Rob., 19
Grevay, My., 20
Gunthorp, Geo., 44; My., 44; Sar., 44
Gunthorpe, Jn., 36*, 37*, 39*, 40, 59*;
 My., 36, 37*, 39, 40, 59; Ric., 39;
 Sar., 40; Wm., 37
Gyniver, Jas., 12, 14; Jn., 12, 14

Hab'rson, Agn., 5; Alice, 5
Hall, Frances, 21; Wm., 21
Hallywell, Eliz., 46
Halsworth, Han., 59*
Handley, My., 49
Hankocke, Jn, 10
Harbey, My., 46; Thos., 46
Harb'rson, Archibald, 4; Rob., 4
Hardy, Dor., 3
Hargreave, Geo., 5; Nic., 5
Harker, Marg., 18; Wm., 18
Haries, Joan, 3
Harison, Ann, 32; Eliz., 32; Ric., 38;
 Sar., 38*; Wm., 32, 55
Harpem, Wid., 60
Harpham, Jn., 49; Rebec., 49; Sus.,
 41, 62; Wm., 41*, 62*
Harson, Cath., 27*, 28*, 47; Chas.,
 27*, 28, 55, 56; Jane, 27; Sar., 27,
 55
Hartshorn, Eliz., 36; Jn., 36; My., 36
Haryson, Eliz., 32; Thos., 32; Wm., 32
Harris, My., 50; Thos., 50
Harrise, Grace, 18
Harrison, Alice, 24, 25; Ann, 24, 26*,
 27*, 28, 29, 37, 45, 51, 52, 53; Dav.,

36, 60; Dor., 39; Easter, 36; Eliz.,
 31, 34, 35, 36*, 37, 50, 56*, 57, 58,
 59; Jn., 26, 27, 43, 51, 52; My., 29,
 33*, 34*, 37, 43, 48*, 52, 57, 60;
 Ric., 28, 35, 36*, 37*, 39, 50, 53, 58,
 59*, 60*, 61, 63*; Sar., 36*, 37*, 39,
 50, 59*, 60, 61, 63; Thos., 27, 33, 35,
 36, 57, 58, 59; Wm., 24*, 25, 26*,
 27*, 28, 29, 31*, 33*, 34*, 45, 48*,
 50, 51, 52, 53, 56*, 57*, 59*, 61, 62
Hathar, Christifoth., 19; Grace, 50
Hather, Ann, 13, 32, 55, 56; Christoph.,
 13, 25; Eliz., 31*, 32, 47, 56; Grace,
 13; Isab., 55; Rob., 31*, 32, 56
Hawkworsth, Rob., 30*
Hawson, Ruth., 21; Thos., 21*
Hay, Ann, 34*, 35*, 36, 49, 58*, 59;
 Anth., 19; Cath., 19*; Geo., 35;
 Humph., 19; Isaac, 35; Jn., 35, 36,
 59; My., 19, 35*, 37; Rob., 34*, 35*,
 36, 49, 50, 58, 59*, 60, 63; Sar., 50,
 60; Thos., 34, 37*; Wm., 35*
Haye, Anth., 17; Eliz., 16; Humph.,
 16; My., 17*
Hayes, Geo., 38; My., 38; Thos., 38
Hayton, Ann, 42; Eliz., 42; My., 39*,
 40; Ric., 41, 62; Sar., 41*, 42*, 62;
 Sus., 39; Wm., 39*, 40, 41*, 42*,
 62*
Haywood, Edw., 57
Heapes, Eliz., 8, 11; Marg., 12; Milli-
 cent, 7, 19; Thos., 7*, 8, 11, 12, 14,
 21
Heaps, Marg., 11; Thos., 11
Heath, Ann, 21, 24; Eliz., 21, 23;
 Joan, 23; Jn., 21*, 23, 24, 25
Heifild, Jane, 2
Henfray, Jarvase, 1; Sar., 1
Henfrye, Jarvis, 9
Henson, Barb., 18; Matt, 18
Herall, Jn., 11
Herison, Ann, 56; Eliz., 32, 33; Jn.,
 32; My., 47; Wm., 32, 33
Hett, Marg., 9
Hewet, Eliz., 44; Geo., 44; Rebec.,
 44
Hewitt, Chas., 44; Geo., 44*; Rebec.,
 44*
Hey, Abig., 4; Debor., 5; Law., 4, 5*;
 Talbott, 5
Heye, Abig., 2; M'r, 5, 9*; Sam., 5, 9;
 Talbot, 9
Heyes, Lawr., 10
Heyfeld, Marg., 2
Heyfield, Ellys, 7; My., 24; Rob., 7*,
 13; Thos., 7, 24; Wm., 24*
Heywood, Alex., 41; Elean., 42; Geo.,
 41; My., 39, 40, 41*, 42, 43*, 62;
 Rob., 40, 62; Sar., 41; Wm., 39*,
 40, 41*, 42, 43, 62

46; My., 26*, 51*; Rob., 24*, 25, 26*, 51*; Troth, 22; Wm., 22, 23, 25

Parnell [Puell], Eliz., 1

Parr, Alice, 47, 58; Ann, 47; Francis, 21; Hy., 21; Jn., 58, 59, 63; My., 19; Wm., 19

Parre, Ann, 15, 20; Bridg., 14; Hy., 14*; Marg., 22; Rob., 20; Wm., 20, 22

Pashlay, Alice, 24

Pashley, Alice, 22; Ruth, 22; Thos., 22*

Patefield, Ell., 45

Peace, Cassandra, 48

Pearson, Eliz., 48; Jn., 48

Peason, Han., 38; Paul, 38; Thos., 38

Peatfield, Ann, 49, 61; My., 49; Wm., 49, 61, 62

Peck, Agn., 1; Jane, 4, 8; Wm., 1, 4

Peck, Ann, 10; Rob., 4; Wm., 4

Pell, Jn., 1; Marg., 1

Penington, Eliz., 46; Wm. 46

Pennington, Eliz., 27; My., 27*, 53*, 54; Wm., 26, 27*, 53, 54, 55

Pernell, Ann, 11

Pettenary, Dor., 19

Pettinar, Dor., 16; Ric., 16*

Pich, Wid., 22

Pick, —, 21; Anth., 21

Pickering, Esth., 47; Marth., 49

Pitche, Isab., 19; Wm., 19

Platts, Dowdghles, 3; Elean., 12; My., 46; Ric., 7; Wm., 3, 7, 12, 46

Pogmore, Ann, 37, 38*, 61; Eliz., 37, 60; Jane, 37; Jonath, 38, 61; My., 36, 40; Matt., 40; Ric., 36*, 37*, 38*, 40, 59, 60*, 61*; Sam., 37; Sus., 36*, 59; Wm., 36, 60

Poole, Eliz., 19; Hy., 19

Pounder, Jos., 49; My., 49

Powell, Sar., 49

Priest, Alice, 48; Jn., 48

Prestwood, Ann, 53; Eliz., 27, 52; Jane, 27, 45, 52; Wm., 27, 45, 52, 53, 54

Pretwell, Eliz., 3; Jn., 3

Rachfild, Alice, 17; Dinas, 17, 19; Dinis, 17; Jn., 17, 19

Rag, Eliz., 48

Ragge, Jn., 3; Sar., 3

Raines, Eliz. 49; Jn., 49

Rashley, Cath., 21; Thos., 21

Ratcliff, Eliz., 40*, 56*; Jn., 56, 60; Ric., 40

Ratcliffe, Ann, 58*; Eliz., 33, 37, 39, 60; Jn., 33, 58, 60; Jos., 58;

Marth., 61; Ric., 33, 37, 39, 58*; Thos., 39, 58; Wm., 37

Ratlief, Eliz., 33*; Jn., 33

Ratlif, Ann, 47; Eliz., 31, 38; Francis, 31; My., 31; Ric., 31, 38*, 47

Ratlife, Ann, 32*; Barb., 56; Eliz., 32*, 56; Jn., 32*, 56; Jos., 32; Ric., 32*, 56; Thos., 32; Wm., 32

Ratliffe, Ann, 33*, 57*; Eliz. 57; Ric., 33*, 57*

Rawood, Epham, 2; Sar., 45, 55; Thos., 2, 45, 55*

Raworth, Eliz., 49

Rawson, Ann, 34*, 41, 57, 58, 63; Bridg., 15, 22*, 52; Eliz., 38, 43, 50; Francis, 34*, 40, 57, 58*, 62; Geo., 44; Marg., 1; Marth., 38, 39, 40, 41, 42*, 43, 44; My., 22, 39; Ric., 34*, 38, 39, 40, 41, 42, 43*, 44, 57; Rob., 15, 22*, 25; Thos., 1, 22; Wm., 43

Rawsone, Bridg., 16*; Rob., 16*; Wm., 16

Rayner, Grace, 1

Reavell, Jas., 63; Sar., 63; Wm., 63

Reavell, Jas., 44, 63; Sar., 44, 63*; Wm., 44, 63

Reavil, Jas., 44; Sar., 44; Wm., 44

Ree, Ann, 54; Edw., 54

Regnalds, Eliz., 45

Remep, Eliz., 20

Renold, Gertr., 2; Hy., 2

Renton, Sar., 49; Wm., 49

Reuel, Alice, 19

Revel, Ann, 50

Revell, Jane, 39; Jn., 39, 60; Sar., 39

Reynolds, My., 48

Rich, Ann, 49; Geo., 49

Richards, Hy., 42; My., 41*, 42, 62; Wm., 41*, 42, 62*

Riche, Thos., 11

Robards, Eliz., 17; My., 17; Wm., 17

Roberts, Benj., 49; My., 49

Robinson, Ann, 39; Eliz., 39*, 46, 48; Wm., 39*, 46

Rocklaye, Isab., 19

Rodgers, Eliz., 48; Theophilus, 48

Roe, Ann, 30; Edw., 29, 30*, 46, 54, 55; Garthurick, 46; Jos., 29; Marth., 30; Wm., 30, 54

Rogers, My., 46

Rooe, Garick, 55

Roson, Bridg., 17; My., 17; Rob., 17

Rotar, Ann, 20

Rouke, My., 47

Rowood, Epham, 10; Thos., 10*

Rowson, Rob., 23; Thos., 9

Russel, Han., 49

Ryley, Marg., 3

Tallbott, My., 2

Tate, Eliz , 19

Taylar, Ann, 22 ; Thos., 22

Tayler, Ann, 25 ; Barb., 12 ; Cuth., 9 ; Eliz., 9, 10; Eshabeth, 2 ; Gartrud, 9 ; Humph., 9, 10* ; Howes, 10 ; Jonath., 12 ; Thos., 25

Taylor, Alice, 3 ; Ann, 22, 49 ; Barb., 14 ; Cuth., 4 ; Eliz., 24, 26*, 44, 45, 52, 54 ; Gartrid., 5 ; Humph., 5; Jn., 26, 52 ; Jonath., 14* ; Raffe, 4 ; Ric., 22, 44, 51 ; Sar., 44 ; Thos., 22, 24, 26*, 45, 51*

Theaker, Eliz., 47

Thompson, Ann, 50 ; My., 46 ; Sam., 46

Thornill, Sar., 44 ; Thos, 44 ; Wm., 44

Thorp, Eliz., 32 ; My., 46 ; Thos., 32 ; Wm., 32

Thorpe, Ann, 31, 34 ; Barb., 47 ; Eliz., 34*, 35*, 39*, 40*, 41, 42*, 48 ; Jn., 31, 34*, 35*, 39, 40 , Marg., 3 ; My., 34 ; Thos., 35, 39*, 40*, 41, 42; Wm , 39, 40*, 41

Thrave, Sar., 46

Tiers, Sar., 47

Tisinton, Ann, 38* ; Eliz , 60 : Han., 38 ; Jn., 60 ; Rob., 32, 33*, 38*, 47, 56* ; Sar., 32*, 33, 47, 56

Tissington, Alice, 44* ; Ann, 36*, 37*, 38*, 39*, 40*, 41*, 42, 50, 61, 62* ; Eliz., 36*, 37, 39 ; Geo., 40, 61 ; Hy., 39, 44 ; Jane, 41 ; Jo., 44 ; Jn., 36*, 37, 38, 39, 40, 41, 42, 44, 61, 62, 63 ; Mark, 36 ; Marth., 40 ; My., 37*, 44, 62 ; Rob., 36*, 37*, 39*, 40, 41, 50, 62 ; Sar., 37, 41 ; Sus. Essex, 39 ; Wm., 42

Tissinton, Ann, 47 ; Rob., 47

Tissiton, Ann, 56 ; Rob., 56

Tod, My., 2, 10 ; Ric., 2, 10, 13

Tomlinson, Ann, 44 ; Eliz., 44 ; Jn., 44

Tompson, Geo., 10 ; Wm., 10

Tomson, Eliz., 2 ; Geo., 7 ; Grace, 7 ; My., 2* ; Wm., 2, 7*

Townerow, Eliz., 3 ; Rob., 3

Trewman, Ann, 13 ; Hy., 12, 13 ; Jn., 12

Trown, Eliz., 39, 40*, 41*, 61* ; Jn., 39*, 40*, 41, 61*, 63 ; Thos., 40, 61 ; Wm., 39, 61

Troown, Eliz., 50, 61 ; Jn., 50, 61

Truman, Hy., 12 ; Marg., 12

Trusswell, Edw., 11 ; Marg., 11

Truswell, Edw., 8 ; Eliz., 11 ; Marg., 8 ; Wm., 10

Trwman, Hy., 12*

Turner, Eliz , 47 ; My., 48

Ulyat (Evlyat, Vllyat), Alice, 47 ; Hy., 32, 47, 56 ; Jn., 32, 37, 38*, 56 ; My., 37, 38* ; Ric., 38 ; Thos., 37, 38

Ulyeat, Alice, 57* ; Hy., 56, 57* ; Jn., 56, 57

Unwin, Eliz., 24 ; My., 42 ; Paul, 42 ; Sar., 42

Upton, Wm., 54

Vrst († Hurst), Agn., 4 ; Jn., 4

Waad, Ann, 2; Jn., 2

Wadgdin, My., 2

Wadson, Chas., 38 ; Hy., 38 ; Jn., 48 ; Marg., 48 ; Milley, 38 ; Rebec., 38

Wakden, Rob., 8

Wakeden, Alice, 1 ; Rob., 4 ; Wm., 1

Waler, Agn., 1 ; Alithia, 5 ; Ann, 11 ; Bridg., 5 ; Hy., 9 ; Joan, 8 ; Jn., 1, 5*, 9 ; Thos., 8

Walker, —, 21 ; Ann, 16, 17, 18, 19 ; Benj., 42 ; Eliz., 36, 42, 44*, 45, 59 ; Jas., 17, 20*, 21, 23* ; Jn., 16, 18, 22, 36, 59 ; Jos., 42 ; My., 16 ; Rosam., 17, 20; Sar., 36, 45, 59 ; Thos., 19 ; Wm. Whiteley, 44

Wallhead, Alice, 21

Ward, Eliz., 41, 42, 44, 45 ; Joan, 9 ; Jn., 9*, 41*, 42, 44, 45, 48 ; Lawr., 44 ; Marg., 9 ; Marth., 48 ; My., 42 ; Thos., 42*, 45, 58 ; Wm., 42

Warde, Jn., 5*; Marg., 5

Wareng, Mawd., 9 ; Rob, 9

Warrener, Ann, 26, 51 ; Cath., 24, 26, 51 ; Chas., 24*, 26, 51*

Warrenr, Cath., 26 ; Chas., 26 ; My., 26

Watkinson, Dor., 63 ; Jn., 44*, 63 ; My., 44

Watmouth, Chas., 8 ; Edw., 8

Watson, Frances, 42*, 63 ; Hy., 36, 38, 39*, 50, 59, 61 ; Jemima, 36, 50, 59 ; Jn., 61 ; Jos., 42 ; Lazarus, 42*, 63 ; Marg., 1 ; My., 36, 45*; Millicent, 38, 39, 61 ; Sar., 42, 63 ; Thos., 1, 39, 45, 55

Wawing, Eliz., 16

We, Hy., 4 ; Ric., 4

Weightman, Ann, 40 ; Jn., 40 ; Sar., 40

Weler, Grace, 10 ; Ric., 10

Welles, Ann, 14 ; Grace, 1 ; Jane, 3 ; Ric., 1, 10 ; Rob., 14 ; Wm., 18

Wells, My., 22, 50 ; Thos., 50

West, Ann, 8 ; Hy., 8*, 48 ; Ric., 8

Whit, Isab., 17 ; Mart., 17 ; Thos., 17

White, Ann, 17, 44 ; Efie, 44 ; Eliz., 22* ; Frances, 18 ; Geo., 22* ; Isab.,